Billy Graham:

Do the Conversions Last?

Billy Graham:

Do the Conversions Last?

By Robert O. Ferm

With Caroline M. Whiting

World Wide Publications
1303 Hennepin Avenue, Minneapolis, Minnesota 55403

BILLY GRAHAM: DO THE CONVERSIONS LAST?

Unless otherwise noted Scripture quotations are taken from the *King James Version* of the Bible.

Scripture quotations marked RSV are taken by permission from the *Revised Standard Version Bible,* copyrighted © 1946, 1952, 1971, 1973 by the Division of Christian Education of the National Council of Churches of Christ in the U.S.A., New York Bible Society.

Scripture quotations marked NASB are taken from the *New American Standard Bible,* © 1960, 1962, 1963, 1968, 1971, 1972, 1973, 1975, 1977 The Lockman Foundation, La Habra, California.

Portions of Chapters 4 and 8 have been excerpted and adapted from *The Psychology of Christian Conversion,* by Robert O. Ferm, © 1959 Robert O. Ferm, Fleming H. Revell Company, Old Tappan, New Jersey.

Library of Congress Catalog Card Number: 88–51050

ISBN: 0-89066-137-5

Printed in the United States of America

Contents

To Lois, my wife, who made this book happen.

Preface

It has been my privilege to have been acquainted with Billy Graham and his ministry for many years. Throughout these years I have learned a great deal from his commitment to evangelism and his commitment in his daily walk with God.

I have tried to make it clear in this book that anytime we talk about conversion we are talking about the Holy Spirit's work in bringing a soul to Jesus Christ. The book focuses on Billy Graham only because his ministry has been a vehicle for the Spirit's work.

But even when we talk about Mr. Graham's ministry, we are not talking about just one man, but about a literal multitude of coworkers as well. Each crusade that Billy Graham has been a part of includes not only the other visible team members, but hundreds of counselors, pastors, prayer partners, and support workers. And many of those who have come forward at the crusades were there in the first place only because of the prayerful and diligent efforts of a church worker, family member, or friend.

Throughout this book I talk about Billy Graham and his ministry. I trust that those who have worked with and prayed for Mr. Graham over the years will realize that I am talking about *their* ministry as well.

Robert O. Ferm

Introduction

About six-and-a-half years ago I knelt in my living room and asked Jesus Christ to come into my heart and be my Lord. I had just watched Billy Graham preach the gospel on TV and ask for people who wanted to give their lives to God.

Now, six-and-a-half years later, my husband and I are campus missionaries. . . . We have been in the ministry full time for three-and-a-half years. We see many people coming to a solid relationship with Jesus Christ and wanting to serve him. We praise the Lord for what he started in our lives through Mr. Graham.

This story is only one of thousands of testimonies from individuals converted through the Billy Graham crusades over the last forty-plus years. Men, women, and children from every continent on the globe have heard Graham preach the gospel since that day in the late autumn of 1949 when the Los Angeles crusade, preceded by numerous smaller but significant crusades, heralded the arrival of a new style of evangelism in an age that perceived mass evangelism to be a phenomenon of the past.

The size and impact of the Graham crusades prompted considerable speculation about the conversion experience on the part of journalists, psychologists, theologians, and sociologists. During the New York crusade in 1957, journalist Sidney Alstrom asked, "What happens under the evangelist's tent?"—a question echoed by literally thousands of people throughout America and around the world. In *The Chicago American*, journalist Harold Fey wrote, "Experience has repeatedly shown that the person who 'accepts Christ' in such circumstances as those seen in Madison Square Garden is very likely to lose his way." This sentiment was embraced by many observers who did not know what actually happened in the crusades. They did not know about the significant and lasting contributions made by crusade converts who were active in the Christian ministry, on the mission field, and in their communities.

Despite the skepticism, however, no one could deny that

something powerful was indeed happening under the evangelist's tent. In the Jewish periodical *Commentary*, Herbert Weiner wrote regarding the New York crusade:

> My friend was not the only one in the Garden that evening who seemed bothered by the calm, uncharged atmosphere of the crusade. The respectability of Billy's evangelism certainly makes it a unique phenomenon in the history of revivalist movements. Yet having said this, we are still left with the question of what has been attracting nearly 20,000 people to Madison Square Garden nightly, for many weeks.

As an associate of Graham, I have had the opportunity to study firsthand, for more than thirty years, the phenomenon of conversion. After I had written a textbook titled *The Psychology of Christian Conversion*, I was asked by Graham to conduct a study of people who had been converted during his various crusades. This book has its roots in that study. Since much of the information was obtained through interviews conducted both orally and through the mail, I have included in chapter 9 a copy of the questionnaire I used. More than 15,000 individuals have completed the questionnaire and/or written unsolicited letters describing their experiences in a Billy Graham crusade. The questionnaires cover a wide range of people and experience, including recent converts as well as some who have been following their call for more than thirty years.

Those who allege that Billy Graham crusade converts are temporary would do well to consider three highly publicized conversions that occurred during the Los Angeles crusade in 1949: Jim Vaus, Mickey Cohen's former wiretapper and a fugitive from the U.S. Army; Stuart Hamblen, songwriter, radio personality, and accomplished horseman; and Louis Zamporini, Olympic pentathlon winner. Each of these famous personalities has been actively serving God since 1949.

Jim Vaus has established schools and retreats for boys and young men in serious trouble with prison authorities in New York and San Diego. By teaching these men the Word of God, witnessing to them, and engaging them in a variety of constructive activities, Vaus has helped to salvage thousands of lives and to forge useful citizens from what appeared to be incorrigible criminals.

Stuart Hamblen turned his songwriting skills and musical ability to producing such famous gospel songs as "It Is No Secret What God Can Do," "This Old House," and many others.

And Louis Zamporini instituted and managed for many years a rehabilitation program for the elderly in conjunction with the ministry of the Hollywood Presbyterian church. Numerous other individuals have remained steadfast in their conversion experiences, and they will be alluded to during the course of this book.

It is important to note that anyone who conducts interviews on the subject of conversion and then interprets the results needs to have experienced the wonder of the new birth himself. Only an inside perspective will allow an author to be sympathetic to the complexities of a conversion that results in life transformation.

Some of the most interesting data resulting from a study of conversion deal with the classes of people who answer the evangelist's invitation as well as the pattern of the conversion experience itself. It might surprise many people to discover that the experiences of those who were converted at a crusade are almost identical to those of individuals converted while watching television or listening to the radio. The pattern, or series of steps, operant on the pathway to a life commitment to Christ are similar—whatever the context. Although most Christians have never experienced such phenomena as the apostle Paul did in his conversion, that is, losing his sight and hearing a voice from heaven, the emotional upheaval and intellectual awakening he experienced are common in many conversions. Thus, it is easy for Christians to identify with Paul, or with St. Augustine, or with St. Francis, or with others who experienced life-changing conversions. The phenomena may vary, but the pattern is the same, as we will note in the conversion stories.

Another important factor to be explored is the historical basis and context for conversion. The Christian church came into being by means of individual conversion—and it continues to grow through individual conversion. Thus, the story of a Billy Graham crusade and of the people who commit their lives to Christ in such a crusade is part of a 2,000-year saga of men and women who have experienced conversion to Christ and have found their place of service in the church.

One of the misconceptions that has plagued mass evangelism through the years is the widespread belief that a conversion experience is brought about by playing on the audience's emotions. None of the major evangelists ever maintained that evangelism was primarily an emotional ministry. John Wesley, George Whitefield, Charles Finney, Jonathan Edwards, Dwight L. Moody, Billy Sunday, and Billy Graham, as well as other evangelical pastors and evangelists, have all maintained that the conversion experience is a response to the message of the Christian gospel. Each one also believed that any emotion evinced in an evangelistic meeting was simply the exuberance and joy that flood those who realize that their sins have been forgiven. The relationship of emotion to the conversion experience will be examined in chapter 4.

To understand what happens in a Billy Graham crusade is to understand the nature of conversion as it is set forth in the New Testament. Both Jesus and Paul presented conversion as a supernatural work of God in the mind and heart of the believer. In his conversation with Nicodemus, Jesus described conversion as a birth from above. Although psychological elements are present in the conversion, it must be understood as the work of God rather than as a psychological construct. Despite the fact that converts quite consistently understand this, not all converted people will be able to explain it to the complete satisfaction of a professional psychologist or psychiatrist. But this inability may be due more to the problem of being inarticulate than to any other cause. An enlightened, articulate believer has no difficulty in explaining precisely what has taken place in his life. He understands that conversion is directly related to the revelation from God that we call the Bible.

It has been written of the great reformers, "They wanted everyone to have the chance to read the Bible because they believed profoundly in its converting power." This statement remains true of great soul-winners in the present day. In his book *The Bible in World Evangelism*, Professor Arthur Chirgwin says, "It seems beyond dispute that the early Christian preachers and writers constantly used the Scriptures as a means of persuading non-Christians to accept the faith." [1] The Bible was the regular tool not only of the early Christian writers and preachers, but also of all the great reformers and evangelists through the centuries.

It is interesting to note, then, that the vast majority of converts in Billy Graham crusades maintain that it was biblical preaching that awakened them. The Word of God rather than their emotions brought them to the point of conversion. Thus, succeeding chapters will show conversion to be not a psychological paradigm nor an emotional indulgence but a simple response to biblical preaching.

Our Creator has fashioned us human beings in such a way that we are capable of, and indeed made for, the experience of conversion. It is both a natural and supernatural process, an occurrence initiated by God and responded to as a result of our inherent capacity for conversion. Sometimes a conversion experience will lead an individual into another religion or perhaps even into a philosophy that does not pretend to be religious—communism, for example. Such a psychological experience may be similar to but never identical with Christian conversion. Any similarities among the many possible types of conversion are the result only of the similarities among individuals, their temperaments, and their responses to stimuli. The differences, however, become more noticeable when one observes the different types of people responding to the gospel. Though the emotional experiences may vary, the actual conversion itself, as well as its results, are the same.

Conversion that is genuine effects a permanent change in an individual, whereas a spurious conversion or one that is psychologically induced proves to be temporary—or reversible. The testimonies which the crusade office has received from 15,000 people, from various countries with various temperaments and various backgrounds, bear witness to the transformation of lives in response to the gospel of Christ. It is my earnest hope that any non-Christian who may be reading this book will someday find an answer to their lingering doubts and to the uncertainties of life and discover the assurance that accompanies a biblical conversion to Jesus Christ.

Since 1949 more than two million people in Billy Graham crusades have indicated their desire to receive Christ. If these individuals had been converts only to Billy Graham, they would never have remained steadfast in their faith and their commitment. But a conversion that is born of the Spirit of God endures. And such conversions take place not only in evangelistic crusades but in thousands of gospel-preaching churches around the world. The following pages invite you to share in the thrilling stories of those who were converted in Graham crusades. Like the testimony that opened this chapter, their testimonies endure, as do their conversions. These are the ones who asked and received, who sought and found, who knocked upon the door and found that it was opened to them.

Chapter One

Who Answers the Invitation?

In every crusade meeting a moment comes toward which all the planning and the preaching, all the singing and the praying, has been directed. This is the moment of decision, the moment when each individual, sitting in the midst of a congregation of thousands, stands alone in the presence of the living God. This is the moment when each man, woman, and child present in the audience is asked to make a personal commitment of his life to Christ. The form of the invitation may vary according to the context and the circumstances, but in each meeting there is the opportunity for an individual to publicly demonstrate his commitment.

Thousands of statistics based on hundreds of worldwide crusades indicate that approximately 4 percent of each audience can be expected to go forward to register a decision for Christ. The Graham team recognizes a fact that is obvious to any observer—that not all individuals who go forward are necessarily converts. Thus, the term *inquirers* was coined many years ago to denote the people who answer Graham's invitation. There are many reasons that people will walk down an aisle at Graham's invitation. Some may come as a result of peer pressure; others to get a closer look at a famous evangelist; still others because their curiosity has been piqued. The vast majority, however, according to their own reports, respond out of a deep desire to have the abundant life that Jesus promises. Tired of the frustration of sinful self-centeredness and a desperate search for fulfillment and satisfaction, many come forward to drink of the fountain of the Water of Life, to assuage their burning thirst.

Just as it is true that not all "inquirers" are necessarily converts, so converts in crusades are not limited to inquirers. One cannot conjecture the ways in which the Holy Spirit moves among those seated in the audience who, for unknown reasons, do not come forward. A public demonstration, although a powerful experience, is not essential for conversion. It is the inward acceptance of truth and one's consequent action upon it that constitutes conversion.

Precisely what an inquirer experiences can never be known by outward observers. It is only in the testimonies, letters, and questionnaire responses—both oral and written—of those who go forward that any degree of insight into the inquirer's experience can be obtained.

A long-range study based upon 15,000 questionnaires, letters, and interviews, conducted over approximately thirty years, reveals that those who have responded to Graham's preaching come from a vast cross section of people around the globe. People from every race, culture, religious affiliation, age group, gender, occupation, educational background, and socio-economic class have answered the invitation to give their lives to Christ. Although a disturbing uniformity may often seem to characterize the local church, diversity is the most prominent characteristic of Graham's crusades.

Invitation Time at Madison Square Garden

It was invitation time one night during the four-month-long crusade at Madison Square Garden in 1957. A middle-aged, distinguished man hurried to the escalator, came down to the main floor of the Garden, and picked his way through and around crowds of people and rows of seats until he stood almost directly in front of the bunting-covered platform where Billy Graham had just concluded a message on the prodigal son. For a brief moment the man stood there alone, apparently not aware of that fact. Graham continued to speak softly, for he had not completed his words of invitation, and in a matter of minutes many other inquirers joined the man.

That night nearly 900 people came to give their lives to Christ, to be released from the oppressive burden of sin. Someone seated on the platform leaned over and whispered, "Isn't it wonderful to see the rich and the poor, the healthy and the disabled, people of all ages and classes, coming together to meet the Savior?" Next to a young polio victim, wheeled to the front by a friend, stood a young couple in shabby clothing. An attractive young woman accompanied by a male friend stood shoulder to shoulder with sixteen Boy Scouts and their scoutmaster. Families came forward together along with a large number of teenagers and GIs. Outwardly they were all different from each other, but each one was expressing the same need—to have his inner emptiness filled by the only thing that can satisfy the human heart—the presence of God. As one young actress said, "I had such a desperate emptiness inside me that at times it actually hurt me physically. I once went to my doctor and asked if he could perform some kind of operation that would ease that gnawing hurt. He told me he could not operate on spiritual problems." But this particular evening at the Garden the Great Physician performed his act of tender surgery, and the suffering of so many lives was healed.

Not far from the platform, where hundreds were standing, waiting quietly to be directed to the counseling room, sat a young reporter. His assignment had been to cover the Graham crusade and to report to the newspapers of the nation. That night he forgot to remain an observer, forgot that a reporter ought not to become involved. Before he realized what he was doing, he had dropped his pencil and was responding to the evening's message which had touched his soul. He ceased to be merely a reporter and became an inquirer and a convert.

Although the reporters who have covered the Billy Graham crusades have always been able to provide nightly statistics to the press, the actual experiences of the inquirers often remained a mystery to them—unless they responded to the invitation themselves. The best they could do was to write a few brief paragraphs about the rallies: "It was a night typical of the seventy meetings Billy Graham has held since he began his crusade on May 15. The 867 inquirers who went forward brought the total to 40,701." This copy was used in one of the many news reports about the New York crusade of 1957.

Of course newspaper headlines reporting attendance figures of 50,000, 80,000, or 100,000 for any given meeting has long since ceased to be astounding news. The Billy Graham counseling teams present at each rally not only provide guidance to each inquirer at the time of the decision but also keep records regarding those who have registered a decision. One reason for the records is to coordinate follow-up procedures with local churches. Another is to maintain an ongoing statistical picture of what happens in the crusades. The percentage of those making a decision for Christ for the first time varies somewhat with each crusade. People also come forward to rededicate their lives to Christ, to receive assurance of salvation, to make a commitment to full-time Christian service, and for other reasons. A Glasgow, Scotland, crusade showed that 79 percent of those coming forward were making a first-time commitment to Christ as Savior. Thirty-four percent of these men and women were church members. Although this data may surprise some people, it is not necessarily atypical of crusade statistics. Church membership and new birth in Christ are not identical terms. Certainly not every church member is a believer, and a number of believers are not affiliated with any church.

One of the highest percentages of first-time inquirers was reflected in a Sydney, Australia, crusade, when 86 percent of those who came forward had never made a previous decision for Christ. One of the lowest percentages was registered in a Nashville, Tennessee, crusade, when only 32 percent of the inquirers were responding to the gospel for the first time.

What Percentage Comes Forward?

What percentage of the audience at a Billy Graham crusade responds to the invitation by coming forward to register a decision for Christ? Let's take a look at some of the statistics. The first set of figures reflects all of the crusades from 1947 through 1987, showing the year, the total number of attendees, and the total number of inquirers.

Year	Number of Crusades	Attendance	Inquirers
1947	2	48,000	1,700
1948	3	65,000	7,400
1949	4	350,000	3,000
1950	6	1,757,000	43,700
1951	8	2,005,550	30,892
1952	7	1,695,330	28,922
1953	8	1,892,030	25,603
1954	5	3,409,933	55,096

Year	Number of Crusades	Attendance	Inquirers
1955	17	4,024,984	115,487
1956	4	2,055,249	49,261
1957	1	2,397,400	61,148
1958	9	2,482,712	81,241
1959	12	3,841,367	160,304
1960	27	1,712,675	67,382
1961	21	2,282,052	62,761
1962	9	1,876,225	50,795
1963	10	1,261,295	45,763
1964	12	1,107,120	54,298
1965	13	1,044,515	35,286
1966	3	1,424,068	52,547
1967	9	1,854,704	69,751
1968	5	1,290,905	56,499
1969	5	1,099,250	50,438
1970	4	1,726,523	43,146
1971	4	1,227,400	48,489
1972	4	1,317,840	34,105
1973	7	4,361,750	123,202
1974	4	1,046,645	48,697
1975	6	1,244,435	57,749
1976	5	1,123,568	43,889
1977	7	1,484,004	48,508
1978	8	1,295,965	41,838
1979	6	1,150,950	48,079
1980	11	695,812	42,762
1981	7	1,026,100	56,300
1982	18	740,350	44,836
1983	4	749,200	27,265
1984	14	2,323,614	111,432
1985	13	1,427,006	85,426
1986	3	543,965	26,003
1987	7	1,046,150	54,064
GRAND TOTALS		65,432,641	2,201,460

These figures not only present an overview of the dates and numbers of crusades held but they also show grand totals of attendees and inquirers. Furthermore, they show that in answer to the question, "Who Answers the Invitation?" an average of 3.4 percent of all those in attendance go forward at Graham's invitation. The statistics for the international crusades (that is, those held outside the United States) reveal that 4.5 percent of those in attendance answer the invitation.

One of the largest crusades ever held by Graham, the four-month-long New York crusade of May to September, 1957, showed these figures: 2,397,400 attendees and 61,148 inquirers, for an inquirer percentage of 2.6. Another large, highly publicized crusade was the Greater London Crusade held from March 1 through May 22, 1954. In this crusade a total of 2,047,333 people attended the rallies, and 38,447 inquirers were registered, for a percentage of 1.9.

Still other statistics on inquirer percentages were compiled for five-day crusades, eight-day crusades, and ten-day crusades. Based on four five-day crusades held in North Carolina and Nevada from 1972 to 1980, statistics show a total of 228,100 in attendance with 12,018 inquirers, for a percentage of 5.3. Eighteen crusades held coast-to-coast in the United States between the years of 1973 and 1985 reflect a total attendance of 3,533,345, with 142,115 people going forward. The percentage of inquirers was 4.0. And finally, five Midwestern and West Coast crusades held between 1971 and 1985 show 1,483,122 people in attendance and 74,974 inquirers, for a percentage of 5.0.

Statistics on Gender and Age

Statistics have also been compiled on the percentages of males and females who go forward in response to the invitation. The overall general statistics for the crusades indicates that approximately 40 percent of the inquirers are male; approximately 60 percent female. Eleven crusades held between 1952 and 1954 showed that 38 percent of the decisions were made by men and 62 percent by women. The percentage of men who went forward in the Greater London Crusade was 34, while that of women was 66. And to look once again at the statistical summaries for the five-day, eight-day, and ten-day crusades: 60 percent of five-day crusade inquirers were women, 40 percent men; 58 percent of eight-day crusades were women, 42 percent men; and 59 percent of ten-day crusades inquirers were women, 41 percent men.

With regard to age, the five-day crusade statistics indicated that 62 percent of those who came forward were twenty-five years of age or younger. Statistics for fifteen crusades of eight-day duration showed that 54 percent were the age of twenty-five or below, and the ten-day crusade figures (for three crusades) indicated that 59 percent were twenty-five years of age or younger. Looking at figures for eleven crusades between 1952 and 1954, we find that of the men responding (38 percent of the total), 21 percent were nineteen to twenty-nine years of age. Twenty-three percent of the women responding (62 percent of the total) were fifteen to eighteen years of age.

The Greater London Crusade figures indicated the following age group breakdowns:

Among Men (34% of the total decisions)

5 - 11	8%
12 - 14	25%
15 - 18	27%
19 - 29	20%
30 - 49	14%
50 +	6%

Among Women (66% of the total decisions)

5 - 11	8%
12 - 14	25%
15 - 18	27%
19 - 29	17%
30 - 49	15%
50 +	8%

The Greater New York Crusade of 1957 showed the following statistics:

Among Men (a total of 20,490 came forward)

5 - 11	8.5%
12 - 14	16.6%
15 - 18	17.5%
19 - 29	19.5%
30 - 49	24.6%
50 +	13.3%

Among Women (a total of 34,393 came forward)

5 - 11	6.3%
12 - 14	14.7%
15 - 18	18.6%
19 - 29	17.4%
30 - 49	26.2%
50 +	16.8%

A random sampling of 400 inquirers who came forward in crusades held throughout the United States, Australia, Canada, Great Britain, Jamaica, and the West Indies showed the following age statistics:

Age	Inquirers
0 - 10	4
11 - 15	32
16 - 20	60
21 - 25	49
26 - 30	38
31 - 35	48
36 - 40	28
41 - 45	29
46 - 50	15
51 - 55	15
56 - 60	16
61 - 65	8
66 - 70	7
71 - 75	3

(Not all respondents to the questionnaires from which this information was taken replied to the question on age.)

All of these figures report a majority of inquirers in the youthful end of the age spectrum. Although we can see some variation in age percentage in the preceding figures, it does appear that if there is one special group that responds with unusual vigor, it is the student group (as we shall see from the statistics on occupations). Certainly individuals who are of a student age are at a time of their life when they are making many critical decisions, even though they are not expertly equipped by experience to do so. Often, however, what they lack in experience they compensate for in their determination to find answers to life's perplexities. This determination, coupled with a hearty sincerity, often produces a quality of commitment that is difficult to find in an adult. Because of the inherent flexibility of youth, major decisions and commitments often do not feel as cataclysmic to young people as they do to older adults. Thus, in spite of the usual turbulence of the adolescent and postadolescent years, conversion often takes place more easily and naturally in younger people than it does in the later years when patterns of life have become well established.

These facts help account for the tremendous interest in Graham and his message on the part of youth everywhere. In London, for example, approximately 70 percent of the people who attended the rallies ranged in age from fifteen to twenty-five. Similarly, in a major crusade in Tokyo nearly 75 percent of the audience were of high school and college age, and the overwhelming response to Graham's message came from that age category as well.

There are certain age groups in almost every crusade that are noticeably absent. Not unexpectedly, one of these groups is young children. Occasionally an eight-year-old or a ten-year-old will come forward at the invitation, but this kind of response among children is infrequent.

Breakdown by Occupation

One of the most interesting statistical breakdowns of crusade response is that of occupation. In the same random sampling of 400 inquirers referred to previously, the following figures emerged:

Occupation	Inquirers
Account representative	1
Accountant	1
Actor	2
Advertising executive	1
Armed services personnel	5
Artist	1
Attorney	1
Auditor	1

Occupation	Inquirers
Auto dealer	1
Babysitter	1
Baker	1
Banker	1
Bookkeeper	5
Builder	1
Bus driver	2
Business executive	3
Carpenter	1
Chef	1
Civil servant	1
Clerk	13
Clothier	1
Coach	1
Commercial artist	1
Construction worker	1
Consultant	1
Counselor	1
Creditor	1
Criminal investigator	1
Dentist	1
Disabled	1
Draftsman	1
Editor	2
Educator	1
Electronics instructor	1
Electronics technician	1
Elevator operator	1
Engineer	2
Expediter	1
Foreman	2
Garment worker	1
Government official	2
Homemaker	70
Income tax consultant	1
Information officer	1
Inspector	2
Insurance agent	4
Juju priest	1
Laborer	20

Occupation	Inquirers
Librarian	1
Machine operator	2
Machinist	1
Maid	4
Mailman	1
Manufacturer's representative	1
Mathematician	1
Medical doctor	2
Mental health worker	1
Microbiologist	1
Midwife	1
Milliner	1
Minister	2
Missionary/evangelist	3
Nurse	6
Nurse's aide	2
Office worker	2
Optician	1
Pharmacist	1
Plant superintendent	1
Plastic molder	1
Policeman	2
Postal clerk	1
Priest	1
Printer	1
Printing contractor	1
Produce examiner	1
Railroad worker	1
Real estate assessor	1
Receptionist	2
Researcher	1
Retired	3
Sales representative	1
Salesman	5
Scholar	1
Secretary	11
Stenographer	3
Student	79
Teacher	7
Television director	1

Occupation	Inquirers
Trade union official	1
Truck driver	1
Typist	3
Unemployed	9
Wine steward	1
X-ray technician	1

As previously noted, the largest single number of inquirers in many rallies is often students, and that fact is also seen in this set of statistics. The second largest group is homemakers. What these statistics reveal most clearly, however, is that great diversity exists within the crusades

Another random sample of 3,000 people showed a high percentage of students as well. The breakdown of figures showed the following: 1,700 students, 480 homemakers, 75 professional women, 90 semiskilled workers, 110 sales and promotion professionals, 300 laborers, 150 retired persons, 60 skilled craftsmen, 18 grade school teachers, 12 high school teachers, a university professor, a medical doctor, a clergyman, an attorney, and a policeman.

A breakdown of inquirers by occupation in a southern United States crusade determined the following: of 17,853 inquirers there were 12,145 students, 1,642 homemakers, 1,480 white-collar workers, 1,478 laborers, 519 professionals, 143 retired and unemployed, 107 military personnel, 36 private entrepreneurs, and 303 without an occupational preference. The pattern in all of the statistics remains fairly constant—with a preponderance of students and homemakers and a vast diversity among other occupations.

Figures on Church Affiliation and Type of Decision

Another variable in the crusades that offers insight about who comes forward is that of church affiliation and/or attendance among inquirers. In the Greater New York Crusade, for instance, 62.8 percent of inquirers said they attended church regularly; 37.2 percent indicated they did not. The London crusade showed that 40 percent of those who came forward were church members; 60 percent were not. Two crusades conducted in the southern United States indicated that 68 percent claimed church membership; 32 percent did not. Approximately 77 percent of inquirers in a large Charlotte, North Carolina, crusade indicated they attended church regularly. It would appear, then, that a fairly large majority of all inquirers already maintained some sort of commitment to a church, although as we have said, church membership and conversion are not identical.

The final set of statistics to be examined regarding crusades deals with the *type* of decision made by an inquirer. Four basic types of responses have been delineated by Graham team members: acceptance or a first-time decision for Christ; rededication of one's life to Christ; assurance or restoration of one's commitment to Christ; and reaffirmation of commitment. In a random sampling of eleven crusades conducted over a two-year period, results indicated that 47 percent of all decisions were from the acceptance, or first-time, category. The Greater London Crusade figures showed that 75 percent of all inquirers were making a first-time decision for Christ. A well-attended Charlotte, North Carolina, crusade showed 30.9 percent of inquirers were making first-time decisions; 20.2 percent were rededicating their lives to Christ; 24.8 percent were reaffirming their faith; and 24.1 percent came forward for assurance. The Greater New York Crusade indicated that for women inquirers, 62 percent of the responses were first-time decisions; 8.5 percent were rededication; 11.8 percent were assurance; 14.1 percent were reaffirmation; and 3.6 percent were for other reasons. For men the figures were: 56.7 percent first-time decisions; 12.3 percent rededication; 11.4 percent assurance; 15.5 percent reaffirmation; and 4.1 percent other.

The statistical summaries for five-day, eight-day, and ten-day crusades we have mentioned before showed a similar pattern as the statistics just cited. Five-day crusades showed 45 percent of all inquirers came forward for acceptance, 38 percent for rededication, 12 percent for assurance, and 5 percent for other reasons. In the eight-day crusades 40 percent said their reason for responding to the invitation was acceptance; 37 percent rededication; 14 percent assurance; and 9 percent other. And finally, the ten-day crusade statistics indicated: acceptance, 45 percent; rededication, 35 percent; assurance, 14 percent; other,

6 percent. All of the accumulated statistics point to the fact that the majority of inquirers were making a first-time decision for Christ, with many expressing a recommitment in some form or other.

Unity in Diversity

As a final way of answering the question, "Who answers the invitation?" let's take a brief, personal look at those who helped constitute the vast diversity that has been seen throughout Graham's crusades.

A personnel director from Cleveland, Ohio, flew to New York specifically to attend one meeting of the crusade being conducted at Madison Square Garden. He came forward to, in his words, "clinch the matter," for he felt that he had unfinished business with God and that this meeting was his personal appointment with Christ.

A man in the foreign exchange business made a decision for Christ because of a statement Graham had made in a sermon on ethical business practices. Soon after his decision, the businessman realized his firm was going to shortchange a client thousands of dollars. He went on record with his objection to the firm's stand, and then even had the courage to resign.

A seventeen-year-old youth came to a crusade meeting because one of his friends had been shot in a gang war the night before. Full of bitterness and revenge, he sought help from a counselor at the podium in dealing with his instinct to take revenge.

A middle-aged couple came forward—the husband to rededicate his life to Christ and the wife to make a first-time decision. In the midst of a separation, this couple had decided to try one more time to make a life together.

An eighteen-year-old came because he had seen one of his buddies in a gang "get converted." He brought a neighbor with him, and they both came forward at the invitation.

A runaway from the Midwest attended the New York crusade as a result of meeting a young woman in a bar one evening. She wanted to attend a crusade meeting, so he unwillingly went along. Captivated by the music, he returned another night and was touched by the message of salvation in Jesus Christ.

A Bible school student came forward to rededicate her life and to ask for prayer for her family that they might accept Christ.

An insurance executive came to a crusade meeting because of curiosity and ended up returning to other meetings, eventually going forward at the invitation.

A Sunday school teacher of six years' duration came forward to receive Christ for the first time. She said her next Sunday school lesson would be sharing her conversion experience.

A bride and bridegroom came forward together to begin their married life with Christ.

A German girl, in the United States for only nine months, came to a crusade out of curiosity about the evangelist. Coming forward, she received counseling from a German team worker.

A university student studying comparative religion came forward to see what the counselors would talk about and ended up giving her life to Christ.

An attorney, interested in the "case for Christianity," found the message speaking not only to his mind but to his heart also.

A Sunday school superintendent of a large church came forward to accept Christ. He realized he had been doing his religious education job mechanically and without inspiration.

And the stories go on and on. The seemingly endless diversity of those who respond to the invitation demonstrates the timeless, universal power of the gospel to transform lives in spite of an infinite array of human variables.*

* All questionnaires and materials from which the statistics in this book were drawn are on file in the Billy Graham Archives at Wheaton College, Wheaton, Illinois.

Chapter Two

"How Can a Man Be Born Again?"

What Is Conversion?

"How can a man be born again?" Few questions have elicited a greater variety of answers and explanations. It was Nicodemus, a devout leader of the Jews, who first posed this question to Jesus. "How can a man be born when he is old?" he asked. "Can he enter the second time into his mother's womb, and be born?"[1] Clearly this well-educated, moral, religious leader had been mystified by Jesus' statement, "Truly, truly, I say to you, unless one is born anew, he cannot see the kingdom of God."[2] And yet Nicodemus had recognized in Jesus "a teacher come from God."[3] He had recognized an authority, a quality of living, an authenticity he had not seen before. He was seeking that which he had not found within the Pharisaic world where he was ensconced, a world that held him in high esteem.

And what was Jesus' answer to Nicodemus? "Truly, truly, I say to you, unless one is born of water and the Spirit, he cannot enter the kingdom of God. That which is born of flesh is flesh, and that which is born of the Spirit is spirit. Do not marvel that I said to you, 'You must be born anew.'"[4]

Modern-day Nicodemuses have asked variations on the same question over and over again. Shortly after Billy Graham began his evangelistic ministry, journalist Lewis W. Gillenson wrote in the July 18, 1950, issue of *Look* magazine: "The question of what, under the revivalist's tent, constitutes a conversion has been wrinkling Protestant brows for 150 years."

Webster defines conversion as "a turning around, a transformation." The *about face* or *turning* implicit in the word conversion is often alluded to in the Bible. Ezekiel admonishes Israel: "Repent . . . and turn away your faces from all your abominations."[5] "Turn to me and be saved, all the ends of the earth! For I am God, and there is no other,"[6] says the prophet Isaiah.

Note that Webster defines conversion as *transformation*, not *reformation*. The new birth is not about resolutions, plans to restructure our lives, or schemes to do better. It is about an interior change that shows all our resolutions, plans, and schemes to be feeble human attempts to do what only God can do—instill a new heart into human beings, so that we become new creations. Only human beings could make conversion a complex matter; Jesus made it simple. He spoke of mustard seeds, of lilies of the field, of grapes and figs, of houses built on rock, of new wine and old wineskins, of wheat and tares. He alluded to everyday tasks and told stories about everyday people.

Conversion is a simple matter, as the apostle Paul pointed out to the Philippian jailer: "Believe in the Lord Jesus, and you will be saved."[7] Such belief is a consciously chosen commitment of one's life, one's self, to Christ. It is not an affirmation of an abstraction, of a concept. It is trust in a person, the Person of Jesus Christ. As a chosen commitment, belief is not dependent on feelings. Assurance of salvation does not rest on *feeling* saved, or forgiven, or joyful.

Because conversion is a radical change from sin to righteousness, it involves the entire person, including intelligence, emotions, and will. Not until all of these aspects are involved can any religious experience be considered to be true regeneration or "new birth." Christian conversion is the enlightened response of the individual, prompted by the Holy Spirit, to the story of God's redemption of sinners through Jesus Christ. Conversion is never *purely* emotional.

A dynamic force in Christian conversion is that of unconscious motivation. The subliminal self, or the subconscious level of thought, contains a great store of memories, thoughts, and desires that may break forth in insights on the level of consciousness. Thus, a religious awakening might occur suddenly, yet be preceded by a long period of unconscious preparation—perhaps involving turmoil and strife.

Swiss psychologist Carl Jung felt that the numerous cultural religious symbols he had discovered were evidence of a "collective unconscious" handed down from generation to generation. Jung believed that this collective unconscious pointed to the fact that humankind is "in search of a soul." This concurs with the apostle Paul's statement, in his address at Athens, that God "hath determined the times before appointed, and the bounds of their habitation; That they should seek the Lord, if haply they might feel after him, and find him, though he be not far from every one of us: For in him we live, and move, and have our being."[8]

Sometimes the seeking, the feeling, and the finding of which the apostle Paul speaks takes most of a lifetime. And yet the profound yearning for God that is our human birthright moves us to discover firsthand that "he [is] not far from every one of us."[9] The sixteen-week New York crusade of 1957 at Madison Square Garden saw more than 61,000 people respond to the preaching of the gospel. One year later 2,400 of them were personally interviewed. One of these was Frank, a sixty-five-year-old New Yorker, who told this story:

All my life I have been groping for something—that's the word, "groping." You see, my mother and father came here from Italy when I was a young boy. They never took me to church. I think my mother's parents did go to church in Italy. My mother was a very good woman. I can still remember how she would emphasize character. She taught me honesty and clean living. She often told me to hold on to God's hand though she never did tell me just what that meant. My father, too, was a good man and of an upright character. I think highly of my parents. They were just like me, always searching for something but never finding it.

When I grew up, I continued to search. I knew something was lacking in my life. But until the first week in June, this year, when I went to the first meeting at the Garden, I had never heard of Genesis or the Bible. I was completely ignorant of what Christianity was. An interesting thing happened to me. I remember last New Year's Day I had made a resolution. I had said to myself, "This will be my spiritual year." I really didn't have any idea what that resolution meant, but I was hopeful. I think even then God was drawing me. I said in my heart that I did want to be a true follower of God.

I waited until June 5 for the answer. I looked at the television schedule and saw that there was a religious program on that night. It was called "Impact." I watched the program and heard some man tell about his religious experience. When the program was ended, I turned off the television. That was something new for me because I was used to watching one program after another. But I felt compelled to call the number they showed on the screen. A fellow by the name of Bob spoke to me. He was so helpful as we talked, and then he invited me to meet him personally at the Garden the next night.

It was on the night of June 6, the next day after watching "Impact" on television, that I went to Madison Square Garden. I went, not knowing that this night would be the night I had longed for and sought for all my life. No one will ever know how I searched for God for many years, and especially for the last twenty years. Nobody ever told me anything about the way to God. I believe that I could not find him because I was not willing to renounce my sins. Now I know that to find God you must be willing to turn away from sin.

When I arrived at the Garden that night, . . . I wanted to meet God. In the taxi I kept saying within my heart, "This is it." I seemed to sense that it was the night when I would come into that beautiful relationship with Christ. I went into the Garden where Bob had reserved a seat for me. I decided that I would listen with an open mind. My heart was open, too, and as Graham spoke, it was as if he was speaking to me. He spoke so simply and yet beautifully about the Savior. He told all about how his death could give me life. I knew through the whole sermon that finally I had found what I had looked for so desperately. Of course I could hardly wait when Billy invited us to come to the Savior. I said as I did on that New Year's night to the Lord, "I do want to be a true follower. I accept thee." I said it as I walked from my seat to the front of the Garden, and the whole experience was indescribably beautiful. I knew that night that I had at last found God. It was really my spiritual year.

Frank is only one of thousands of men, women, and children who have experienced a turning around, a transformation, often after a long time of searching. Their testimonies cannot be captured inside the confines of a particular definition of the word *conversion*. All that can truly be said of their experience is found in the statement of the blind man whom Jesus healed: "One thing I know, that, whereas I was blind, now I see."

Kerygma: The Content of Conversion

We have said that conversion is a turning around, a transformation. Now, we may ask, a turning from what to what? Whatever definition *conversion* may be given, we must note that *Christian* conversion implies a turning away from sin toward the acceptance of a particular message—a specific content. There is no such thing as a Christian conversion without the conviction that Jesus Christ, through his victory on Calvary, secured humankind's eternal redemption through his self-sacrifice. Without the acceptance of, the belief in, this content, conversion would be nothing more than an emotional response to a temporary stimulus—without the enduring qualities of the new birth and an awareness of being accepted into the family of God. Romans 8;16 says, "The Spirit itsclf beareth witness with our spirit, that we are the children of God." Such knowledge is part of Christian conversion.

On occasion, critics of mass evangelism in general, and of Graham in particular, have insinuated that those who go forward at crusades do so only as a knee-jerk response to an emotional stimulus. Such allegations overlook the centrality of the solid content of preaching in the conversion experience. This involves the acceptance of certain historical data—as well as the relationship of those data to one's *personal* situation. Indeed, conviction that Jesus Christ has come into the world to save sinners lacks saving efficacy unless one *personally* appropriates the benefits of his atonement. Only when the truth is internalized does it become a means of transformation.

One of the criticisms leveled at Graham's crusades, because of the sizable numbers of people who visibly respond, is that those who go forward do so as part of a mass movement. In all the questionnaires and testimonies that have been received by Graham and his associates, not one convert has ever given the impression that he or she felt reduced to being part of a mass movement. Testimony after testimony has indicated that at a certain point in the meeting, while listening to Graham's message, the potential converts felt themselves to be virtually alone in hearing the message of Christ.

Although no legitimate Christian conversion can ever occur without response to specific content, the content cannot accomplish spiritual transformation if it is received merely by the intellect. Full appropriation of the gospel message occurs only when the will has been surrendered *as a result* of deeply hearing that message. The act of surrender involves both an *experiencing* and an *experienced* quality, as Wheeler Robinson has pointed out in *The Christian Experience of the Holy Spirit*. "When Billy began to preach," said one convert in a major crusade, "we were both suddenly aware of the fact that something was happening to us that we couldn't explain. . . . I felt a power working in my soul that I couldn't resist." Another convert describes the experienced/experiencing quality this way: "I don't know how to explain to you what took place, but right while I was confessing my terrible need, and asking God for help, I was mysteriously led to put my whole trust in Christ. I was helped to rely on what he had done for sinners."

The Christian conversion experienced by these two is defined in Scripture as the human response to the *kerygma,* or theological content, of the gospel message. This *kerygma,* says the apostle Paul, is: "Christ died for our sins according to the scriptures; And . . . was buried and . . . rose again the third day according to the scriptures."[10] Paul furthermore says, "This is the message you have received, and wherein you stand, by which also you are saved." There is no other message, according to the New Testament. While the church was concerned with the teaching of the Lord, it was not by teaching that it made converts. It was by *kerygma,* says Paul, not by *didache* (teaching), that "it pleased God to save men."

It follows, then, that any truly converted person will have experienced a response to this specific theological content; such a content will have been essential to conversion. And this fact is true not only of Billy Graham crusades, but also of all evangelical preaching. Subsequent to conversion, believers partake of what is termed *didache*—the larger body of Christian teaching that interprets the full range of responsibility one assumes as a member of the body of Christ. Once again, it is the content that distinguishes Christian conversion from mere psychological conversion. The "preaching of the cross," as Paul says in 1 Corinthians 1:18, teaches Christ's crucifixion, burial, and resurrection; all parts of the finished work of Christ for sinners. The cross, says Paul, is to us who "are saved . . . the power of God."

Controversy has often been provoked by those who pit the content of conversion against the faithful, feeling response to this content. It is important to recognize the balance between these two factors of the conversion experience. If the intellectual grasp, the understanding, of the *kerygma* is separated from the moment of crisis, the feeling of God's inner call, then the balance is lost. The result is either a type of confessionalism without personal knowledge, or an existential leap lacking in content. Neither pole is likely to issue in the true Christian life.

It is important to note, however, a point that Graham has made in his book *How to Be Born Again*:

> . . . how kind and understanding and compassionate God has been in choosing to reveal Himself to man through simple childlike faith rather than the intellect. There would otherwise be no chance for little children or the mentally retarded or brain damaged. And yet the brilliant scientist, the true intellectual, the genius, must all come the same way. As Jesus said in Matthew 18:3, "Unless you are converted and become like children, you shall not enter the kingdom of heaven."
> The gospel message doesn't have to be understood by the seeking soul, only to be received in simple faith. [11]

The Word of God and Conversion

Because the *kerygma* is constant and unchanging, not dependent upon the evangelist, many of those who attend Graham's rallies report that as they listen to the preaching of the Word, they find they have forgotten the speaker. One man who went forward says:

> Graham quoted the verse that says, "For there is one God, and one mediator between God and men, the man Christ Jesus; who gave himself a ransom for all. . . . " This I simply could not refute. This was the gospel according to any translation or version of the Scriptures. It was this use of the Scriptures that was the deciding factor because I was put in the position of either accepting the authority of the Scriptures or rejecting it. It was not a controversy with Billy Graham. By his use of the Scriptures, he removed himself from the center and put God and the Scriptures there instead.

Testimony after testimony has born witness to the fact that while emotion has been present in conversion experiences, it was not emotion that prompted any convert's decision. Rather, it was a confrontation with the truth of the gospel. This confrontation brought about repentance and faith, resulting in a total commitment to Christ. But it was the *kerygma* that existed, like bedrock, prior to the other aspects of the experience of full salvation. All true gospel preaching possesses both information and inspiration.

History clearly shows the vital relationship between the Bible and evangelism. In *The Bible in World Evangelism* A. M. Chirgwin says, "The Bible confronts men with Christ and brings them to a decision."[12] The reason for the relationship between evangelical conversion and the Bible is clear: "The very concreteness of the Bible, as something that can be seen and handled, has not been a hindrance but a help," Chirgwin continues. "It has been a constant corrective of that kind of subjective interpretation that is based on the theological views or personal idiosyncrasies of the individual."[13]

Many individuals have recognized this compelling power in the Scriptures. In *The Wonder of the Word*, G. M. Day noted: "When one reads the Bible and finds growing within himself a sense of God and eternal values, a new perspective on life, a hungering and thirsting after righteousness, an impulse to holy living, and a divine constraint to self-relinquishment and sacrificial service, he knows that God has dealt with him through its message."[14]

It is the sense of certitude that the Bible begets, which no other written record can parallel, that displays its uniqueness and power. Martin Luther exclaimed, "My conscience is captive to the Word of God." Multitudes of men and women who have experienced classic conversions agree. It was through reading Romans 13:14 that St. Augustine experienced conviction of his sins and entered into a life of service. Having escaped the relentless grip of sin and having fled to the freedom found in Christ, Augustine exulted in his newfound faith and deliverance.

In this age of high technology and scientific advances, it is amazing to discover that the Word of God has not lost its compelling power. Thousands of those who have gone forward at Billy Graham crusades have reported that it was the Word of God itself, not the evangelistic techniques of the Graham team, that impelled them to a decision for Christ. Similar responses have been reported among a wide spectrum of those who came to the meetings—whether they were Hindu or Moslem, Confucianist or Shintoist, Baptist or Episcopalian. For example, Matsuyo Shiratori, a forty-seven-year-old mother of four and daughter of a Shinto priest, heard the gospel for the first time at a Graham rally in Tokyo. Instrumental in her attendance at the crusade was this verse, which she saw in the home of a dying friend: "I am the way, the truth, and the life: no man cometh unto the Father, but by me".[15] Such simple, unembellished words from the gospel have moved countless others to make the most important decision of their lives—the decision for Christ.

Chapter Three

The Biblical Prescription for Conversion

In addition to being the compelling force for conviction of sin and of salvation in the lives of men and women from every land, the Bible prescribes the method and process of conversion and portrays conversion as the normative way of bringing individuals to Christ. Whenever the New Testament speaks of conversion, it is not as a novelty or an innovation, but as the normal means of giving people the confidence and hope promised by the Scriptures and drawing them into the church of Christ.

To establish the validity of any evangelistic endeavor, this question must be asked: Does the experience taking place in the lives of the converts correspond to the New Testament formula? The New Testament abounds in references to conversion. John the Baptist opened his ministry with a stern call to repentance. His ministry was preparatory to that of Jesus, but it brought the issue of conversion to the attention of the people. John's brief but spectacular ministry called for conversion in no uncertain terms. No less emphasis was placed on conversion by Jesus, who described the experience as a "new birth" or as being "born from above." Psychologist William James described the conversion experience in similar terms: "A self hitherto divided, and consciously wrong, inferior, and unhappy, becomes unified and consciously right, superior, and happy."[1] It is precisely this transformation that has characterized the entire history of the church—wherever real conversion has occurred.

There are four steps that the Bible describes as part of the conversion process. The first is *recognition* of God's gift of his Son, who loves us so much that he died on the cross. In the Book of John we read, "For God so loved the world, that he gave his only begotten Son, that whosoever believeth in him should not perish, but have everlasting life."[2]   In Galatians we read, "The Son of God . . . loved me, and gave himself for me."[3]

According to the New Testament, the second step is *repentance* of sins. In Mark we read, "Repent, and believe."[4]   In Luke Jesus says, "Unless you repent you will . . . perish."[5]

The third thing God asks of us is to *receive* Jesus Christ as Savior and Lord. We read in John, "But as many as received him, to them gave he power to become [children] of God, even to them that believe on his name."[6]   Trusting Christ absolutely means that we acknowledge we cannot save ourselves.

Confessing Christ publicly is the fourth step, according to the Bible. Taking a stand, establishing a witness, reinforces a new convert in his or her newfound faith. Jesus said, "Everyone therefore who shall confess Me before men, I will also confess him before My Father who is in heaven."[7]

Any genuine conversion—whether it occurs during an evangelistic rally or in some other context—will reflect the four steps described above. Many converts, in both crusades and local churches, report that they suddenly had an insight or a keen understanding of the essential truth of the Christian gospel. This factor of *recognition* has long been noted by theologians as well as by certain psychologists. Carl Jung, for example, spoke of an intellectual upheaval that produced conflict, often resulting in a genuine conversion experience.

Those who hold to the authority and dependability of the Scriptures recognize that conversion usually involves a moment of crisis. Every incident of conversion in the New Testament illustrates this crisis—manifest in the radical internal change that takes place in the new birth. As we have noted, it is the *kerygma* that effects this crisis in the individual. Frequently a period of storm and stress precedes this conversion crisis—during which men and women become acutely aware of, and seek release from, the sin in their lives. In his *Systematic Theology*, Augustus H. Strong has written:

> [Conversion] is an instant change. Regeneration is not gradual work. Although there may be a gradual work of God's providence and Spirit preparing the change and a gradual recognition of it after it has taken place, *there must be an instant of time when, under the influence of God's Spirit, the disposition of the soul, just before hostile to God, is changed to*

> *love.* Any other view assumes an intermediate state of indecision, which has not moral character at all, and confounds regeneration either with conviction or with sanctification. [8]

A recurring pattern seen in converts who have come forward at Billy Graham rallies indicates that, first, an event or circumstance disrupts the individual's established pattern of thought. Second, the individual is confronted with certain claims or demands. Third, they grasp the core of the gospel. Fourth, the moment of crisis occurs. And fifth, certain characteristics are evident in the newborn person.

A study of those who came forward reveals that, although there are numerous variations in the details of the converts' life stories, there is little variation in their description of the moment of conversion—a moment characterized by the immediacy of truth. All of a sudden one feels convicted of sin and is aware of the rebellion that exists in the human heart. Faith is experienced, not as a virtue of the individual, but as a gift from God.

One convert who shared her story wrote:

> It was on a Saturday night when we were watching television that I first heard Billy Graham. I thank God that they had that program on TV or I might not ever have heard anything about it. I was glued to the TV set for that hour, and after it was over I just couldn't look at another program that night. It seemed too sacred. God had spoken to me.
>
> I decided to go and hear Billy in person, so the next free night I had, I went. You can't believe the change that took place. I can't remember any particular Scripture Billy quoted, but he did make the way to Jesus clear. . . . All of a sudden I received hope and was encouraged to leave my seat and go down to the front to be born again. It all happened just as Graham said. He said that a person could go home completely changed. I did.

Numerous historical examples exist of a disruptive event in the life of a potential convert: a thunderstorm and the death of a close friend in the life of Martin Luther; a storm at sea in the life of John Wesley, and the stoning of Stephen in the life of the apostle Paul.

In a follow-up study a number of converts were asked, "Can you remember any unusual event prior to your conversion that stimulated serious thought or concern over spiritual matters?" All of the adults who responded indicated that some particular occasion stimulated serious thought on spiritual matters—

thought which later led to a decision. The death of a close friend or family member, a powerful dream, an eloquent sermon, a significant historical event, for example, served as catalysts for subsequent conversion. A significant catalyst is often the preaching of the Word, which can create a powerful disturbance in thought and behavior patterns, so that one is compelled to search for a spiritual answer to life's problems.

Second, an individual is confronted with claims and demands that call for a decision. Although the person may have been aware of these claims prior to the time of crisis, at the moment of decision they demand a new response.

Third, the core of the gospel is grasped; namely, one realizes that he is a sinner, that Christ has died for him, and that salvation is available to him through Christ's completed work. Among converts surveyed, the Scripture verse most often quoted was: "For the wages of sin is death; but the [free] gift of God is eternal life through Jesus Christ our Lord."[9] It is evident that regeneration is brought about through the activity of the Spirit, as he brings the Word of God to bear upon the mind of the individual. It is to be expected, then, that the person experiencing the crisis of regeneration will have some conception of the *content* of his belief. In fact, the crisis is the reaction to specific truth when the mind is activated through the influence of the Spirit. Again, converts surveyed indicated that their decision, which issued in a crisis, was based upon objective facts presented for apprehension by faith.

Fourth, the pattern among those who told their conversion story was that there was a specific, decisive moment, a moment of crisis, when they made a definite, clear decision that transformed their lives. Certainly the conversions recorded in the New Testament occurred at a particular, observable time. Perhaps the most notable conversion recorded in the Bible, that of the apostle Paul, is remarkable for its specificity of time and place:

> As he journeyed he approached Damascus, and suddenly a light from heaven flashed about him. And he fell to the ground and heard a voice saying to him, "Saul, Saul, why do you persecute me?" And he said, "Who are you, Lord?" And he said, "I am Jesus, whom you are persecuting; but rise and enter the city, and you will be told what you are to do."[10]

The fifth aspect of the pattern reflects the immediate results of the conversion crisis. As the Scriptures tell us, peace and joy issue from the decision, men and women are turned "from darkness to light, and from the power of Satan unto God,"[11] and, "Like as Christ was raised up from the dead by the glory of the Father, even so we also should walk in newness of life."[12] Sometimes people confuse the results of the conversion with the actual conversion experience, but this confusion may be understandable in light of the new converts' insufficient knowledge of Scripture and their infancy in the spiritual life.

As Graham points out in *How to Be Born Again*:

> The contrasts used in the Bible to express the change which comes over us when we are born again are very graphic: from lust to holiness; from darkness to light; from death to resurrection; from stranger to the kingdom of God to now being its citizen. The Bible teaches that the person who is born again has a changed will, changed affections, changed objectives for living, changed disposition, new purpose. He receives a new nature and a new heart. He becomes a new creation.[13]

One of the most noteworthy results of conversion is the change wrought in the understanding of the converted person. In Ephesians we read that Paul prayed:

> That the God of our Lord Jesus Christ, the Father of glory, may give unto you the spirit of wisdom and revelation in the knowledge of him: The eyes of your understanding being enlightened; that ye may know what is the hope of his calling, and what the riches of the glory of his inheritance in the saints, And what is the exceeding greatness of his power to us-ward who believe, according to the working of his mighty power.[14]

A second distinguishing characteristic common to those who have experienced the evangelical crisis is the evident submission to the will of God. This new way of being is caused not by emotional coercion, but by the willing disposition of the soul to yield itself to Christ, whereupon Christ works according to "his good pleasure."[15]

The Scriptures cite particular evidences of conversion. Keeping God's commandments indicates a changed life: "And hereby we do know that we know him, if we keep his commandments."[16] Another characteristic of those who have experienced a conversion crisis is that they love others: "We know that we have passed from death unto life, because we love the brethren."[17]

The relationship of the believer to the world changes dramatically after conversion. In 1 John it says, "Love not the world, neither the things that are in the world. If any man love the world, the love of the Father is not in him."[18] One also experiences victory over the world: "For whatsoever is born of God overcometh the world: and this is the victory that overcometh the world, even our faith. Who is he that overcometh the world, but he that believeth that Jesus is the Son of God?"[19]

The Holy Spirit and Conversion

Nearly every preacher of the gospel is aware that however often he may emphasize the message of the cross, there will be those listening who did not hear. He will also note that there are those who both heard and responded when the Good News was shared with them. Reflection upon these truths will indicate that an unpredictable factor exists in all true conversion; namely, the Holy Spirit. The gospel says, "The wind bloweth where it listeth, and thou hearest the sound thereof, but canst not tell whence it cometh, and whither it goeth: so is every one that is born of the Spirit."[20]

That there is a direct relationship between the operation of the Holy Spirit and the presence or absence of the *kerygma* seems certain. An exaggerated concern with the communication of the Christian message is unnecessary. What is important is the proclamation of the Good News and then abandonment of the results to the work of the Holy Spirit. It is the Spirit who applies to the individual the truth of the Word that results in regeneration. The Spirit indwells at the instant of regeneration, quickening the natural powers of the convert and transforming him. In confirmation of this fact, the New Testament points out that the Spirit is indwelling: "But you are not in the flesh, you are in the Spirit, if in fact the Spirit of God dwells in you."[21]

This occupation of the human personality by the Spirit of God is the explanation of the newness of life essential to every believer. This phenomenon might be described as the invasion of an individual's personality by a second personality, which lives effectively through the renewed being. The result of this invasion of one's entire personality by the Spirit of God is "Christ in you, the hope of glory."[22]

In *The Doctrine of the Holy Spirit*, George Smeaton suggests that the Spirit's mode of activity may be compared with the wind. He cites these parallels:

> (1) The Spirit's agency is sovereign, like the wind blowing where it will; (2) The mode of his activity is inscrutable; it is like the wind, in regard to which we can neither say where it begins to blow nor where it is hushed to rest; (3) The efficacy is irresistible, and the effects indubitable; we hear the sound thereof. [23]

Biblical Accounts of Conversion

Numerous stories appear in the Bible telling about men and women from all walks of life who encountered Jesus and were then irrevocably changed. The Samaritan woman, who as a prostitute was an outcast in her own village, met Christ at the well during the heat of the day, when she knew she would not meet other villagers. She was changed in the twinkling of an eye, rushing home to tell the Good News of Christ. We read in the Book of John, "Many of the Samaritans believed on him because of the word of the woman who testified, 'He told me all the things that I have done.'"[24]

A dramatic change was seen in Zacchaeus, a dishonest tax collector. Short in stature, he had climbed a tree to see and hear Jesus preach. Instantly changed as a result of his encounter with the message of Christ, he repented and decided to make restitution for his wrongdoing: "Behold, Lord, half of my possessions I will give to the poor, and if I have defrauded anyone of anything, I will give back four times as much."[25]

Matthew's gospel account tells us about the immediate, wholehearted response of two sets of fishermen brothers, Peter and Andrew, and James and John. "Follow me, and I will make you fishers of men," said Jesus. "And they straightway left their nets and followed him."[26] And we have already mentioned the dramatic conversion of Saul, zealous persecutor of Christians.

In terms of size, perhaps the most spectacular conversion experience cited in the New Testament was the dramatic change that took place in 3,000 people on the day of Pentecost: "Suddenly from up in the sky there came a noise like a strong, driving wind which was heard all through the house where they were seated. Tongues as of fire appeared, which parted and came to rest on each of them. All were filled with the Holy Spirit."[27] Such was their exuberance that bystanders accused the new converts of having had too much new wine!

Biblical Terms Relating to Conversion

Although *conversion* is the primary word used to describe the observable transformation that takes place in the individual who responds to the gospel of God's grace, numerous other terms are used in the Bible to describe some aspect of salvation through Christ. It is interesting that whenever conversion is referred to in the New Testament, the Greek verbs used to describe the experience are of the *aorist* tense. This is the tense that indicates an action that has occurred once and for all. Conversion is a once-and-for-all matter.

Among the terms used in the Bible to connote the conversion experience are *saved, born again, born from above, made alive, justified*, and *redeemed*. Jesus used the expression *born from above*[28] to describe the supernatural character of the new birth. Peter referred to being *born from above*,[29] differentiating the spiritual birth from the physical birth. On the occasion of Pentecost, Peter used the Old Testament term *saved*, a word found frequently throughout the Book of Acts.[30] *Saved* was also used by Paul in his more theological and polemical writings.[31]

Other terms include *made alive, regeneration*, and *justification*.[32] *Regeneration* connotes a new life infused into the individual, while *justification* refers to the legal standing that the believer has before God, inasmuch as his sins have been judged and dealt with not on his own merit but according to the merit of Jesus Christ. *Justification* is closely related to the idea of substitution, in which the sinner goes free because of what another has done in his place.

Readers of the Gospel of John will be impressed by the repetition of the word *receive*—twenty-eight times, and the word *believe*—ninety times. Paul uses *faith* thirty-seven times in Romans, which is usually considered to be the Bible's most complete treatise on the process of salvation. *Faith* occurs in

Galatians twenty-two times. Hebrews also refers to *faith*, a key word in the experience of conversion, twenty-two times.

Faith and Conversion

What is faith? The belief that Christ was who he claimed to be, and that he could do what he promised; that is, forgive sins and transform lives. The author of the Letter to the Hebrews says: "Without faith it is impossible to please him: for he that cometh to God must believe that he is, and that he is a rewarder of them that diligently seek him."[33] Faith involves all the capacities of the human—the intellect, the emotions, and the will. It is an act of commitment and a conscious choice to follow Christ. The Bible points out that it is impossible to please God without faith. One aspect of faith is surrender, the giving of oneself completely to God. It is our response to his offer of forgiveness and mercy. Faith is not just a concept; it is trust in a specific person—Jesus Christ. And faith is not dependent on our *feeling* saved. It transcends our capricious emotions.

As Graham has written, "A person cannot be coerced, bribed, or tricked into trusting Jesus. God will not force His way into your life. The Holy Spirit will do everything possible to disturb you, draw you, love you—but finally it is your personal decision."[34]

Repentance and Conversion

The word *repentance* is found in the Old Testament forty-three times and in the New Testament fifty-five times. In the Book of Acts we read that Paul says, "The times of ignorance God overlooked, but now he commands all men everywhere to repent."[35] Of Jesus, we read that "repentance and remission of sins should be preached in his name among all nations."[36] *Repentance* speaks of a change of mind, an admission that one is a sinner, and that Jesus has accepted full responsibility for one's sins. It also means a change of mind about the justice of God in removing condemnation from sinners through Christ's act of atonement. It means a change of mind about the Person of Jesus—arriving at seeing him as the unique fulfillment of all the promises of God to his people.

To quote Graham once again:

Repentance is *first*, and absolutely necessary, if we are to be born again. It involves simple recognition of what we are before God—sinners who fall short of His glory; *second*, it involves genuine sorrow for sin; *third*, it means our willingness to turn from sin. [37]

What Happens After Conversion?

Subsequent to conversion, the rates of growth in Christian maturity vary according to individuals. Just as physical maturity takes time, requiring adequate nourishment, exercise, and rest, so spiritual growth requires its own kind of nourishment—or malnutrition will set in! The new convert is like a baby who constantly demands milk, but is not yet ready for solid food. There are several specific ways a beginner in the Christian life can cultivate growth.

First, one must faithfully read and study the Word of God. Although much of what a new convert reads may be unclear at first, enlightenment will come as one continues to read with the eyes of the heart. Romans 15 says, "For whatever was written in former days was written for our instruction, that by steadfastness and by the encouragement of the scriptures we might have hope."[38] Committing Bible verses to memory can be a great fortifier in times of distress. This practice also encourages a convert to spiritually digest portions of the Scriptures that feed the inner person.

The apostle Paul counseled the Thessalonians to "pray without ceasing."[39] Likewise, Jesus said, "Men ought always to pray."[40] Although a new convert may feel awkward addressing God for the first time, he can remember that one can talk to God just as a child talks to a loving parent. Fluency and eloquence are not important; sincerity and honesty are. And the more specific one's prayers are, the better. Platitudes and generalities are not personal, and God is interested in us as *individuals*.

A Historical View of Conversion

Some twentieth-century observers of religious movements and phenomena have claimed that mass conversions were characteristic of former times but are not to be expected in our own times. Of course the success of the Billy Graham crusades has tempered this viewpoint of one of the most unpredictable factors in the history of Christianity—the revival.

Revival meetings have been exceedingly important in the history of Christianity. Although conversion is certainly not limited to mass meetings (conversions take place regularly in gospel-preaching churches throughout the world), such meetings have had an undeniable impact. The Wesleyan revival in England, the Great Awakening in New England, the preaching of Dwight L. Moody, Billy Sunday, Charles Finney, George Whitefield, Charles Haddon Spurgeon, and other less well-known evangelists have contributed to a tradition of mass evangelism that has transformed uncounted lives. It is unfortunate that stereotypes of fast-talking preachers have demeaned the image of genuine, gospel-preaching evangelists. The movie "Elmer Gantry," for example, cast a cloud of suspicion and doubt upon revivalists in general.

In any event, the closest scrutiny on the part of his severest critics has revealed Graham to be irreproachable in his ministry. As A. C. Underwood wrote in his book *Conversion: Christian and Non–Christian*, "Conversion is not simply a lingering superstition among certain sects, but an undeniable fact, occurring at all periods in the history of the Christian church."[41] And it is impossible not to take seriously the record numbers of authentic, validated conversions that have resulted from Graham's worldwide crusades.

Christian Conversion Distinguished From Other Conversions

"Faith always implies an object—that is, when we believe, we must believe something. That something I call the *fact*,"[42] writes Graham in his book *Peace With God*. It is precisely the truth revealed in this statement that manifests the uniqueness of evangelical Christian conversion.

It is written in the Scriptures concerning the children of God, "The world knoweth us not, because it knew him not."[43] Again it is written, "The world cannot receive [him], because it seeth him not, neither knoweth him."[44] If Christ is present and active in regeneration, and absent in merely psychological conversion—or conversion in non-Christian religions—then the non-converted cannot speak authoritatively about the experience of Christian conversion.

Careful attention to the details of the conversion crisis indicates that there is, indeed, a uniqueness in the crisis as experienced by the evangelical. This uniqueness does not lie in a person's psychological constitution; all religions and some philosophies grant to their followers some form of satisfaction in religious experience. Even the New Age movement reports satisfying moments of euphoria experienced by spiritual seekers. The uniqueness, then, lies in the *content* of what is believed. This fact does not readily reveal itself to the psychologist, for even those who are sympathetic have found it to be a difficult task to get a subject to willingly lay bare his inner and sacred experiences with God for the purpose of psychological analysis.

Of course one's conclusion usually depends upon the starting point. If an observer, particularly a clinical psychologist, begins with observation of the natural phenomena in the conversion experience, then the almost unavoidable conclusion is that conversion is a psychological phenomenon. This conclusion would warrant the belief that, as a psychological phenomenon, conversion is common to many religions and that there is no uniqueness in any of them, even the Christian experience. The evangelical conversion experience does have some of the psychological concomitants of the other experiences. This fact, however, is merely evidence of the basic truth that *human beings are capable of being converted*. People are converted and counter-converted to all major religious traditions—and to ideologies (for example, communism) as well.

Psychologists are well aware that human beings experience conversion in a variety of ways. Even psychological treatments and psychotherapy are intended to induce conversion of a certain kind. A synthesis of the many definitions in various studies of religious psychology has led to an acceptable general definition: conversion is a kind of psychological surrender to an ideal that will result in a moral change. Such a change would not approximate that which characterizes the Christian life, but many non-Christian conversions have brought about at least some moral improvement. The type of conversion sought for through Alcoholics Anonymous, for example, is expected to produce the moral improvement of abstinence from the use of alcohol.

The kind of conversion characteristic of Hinduism presents a remarkable parallel to the Christian experience in certain respects. In Hinduism the surrender is made to Siva, Rama, or Krishna. Such surrender to an ideal can also be found in the religions of other lands, but it is particularly evident in some of the more mystical spiritualities.

Although we have already noted that a great gulf intervenes between the nature and result of the Christian and the non-Christian conversion experiences, it must be reiterated that a universal psychological likeness exists. Either the surrender of the self to the ideal occurs or no conversion can take place. Such an ideal is defined by Gordon Allport:

> A man's religion is the audacious bid he makes to bind himself to creation and to the Creator. It is his ultimate attempt to enlarge and to complete his own personality by finding the supreme context in which he rightly belongs. [45]

The ideal may be an intellectual one or an affectional one, but there must be surrender. This capacity of human beings to surrender self is turned inward, a conscious or unconscious attempt being made to find satisfaction. The ability to experience conversion is such an integral part of the human personality that men and women are persistent in their craving for spiritual fulfillment—through whatever means.

Thus, conversion is the turning outward from the self to an "other" and making personal commitment to that other. This psychological principle constitutes the framework for the experience. The psychological mechanism of the individual makes the surrender possible, and until this change has taken place, he fails to discover his fulfillment.

Chapter Four

Emotions and the Conversion Experience

A number of critics of mass evangelism in general, and of Billy Graham in particular, have expressed the opinion that evangelists often take unfair advantage of the emotions of the audience. Many people, including both proponents and opponents, believe that conversion almost inevitably involves a tremendous emotional upheaval. The assumption that most of the people attending a crusade are highly susceptible to emotional stimuli feeds this belief. The aura of mystery and drama that people project onto the conversion experience often gives a false representation of an authentic response to the gospel message.

Certainly the history of evangelism reveals that there have been "revivalists" who resorted to illegitimate methods in order to elicit audience response. The "Elmer Gantry" phenomenon has cast aspersions on the validity of the authentic evangelists. Of course the results of purely emotional appeals are anything but satisfactory or enduring. Resorting to pure emotionalism is a cheap trick used by preachers who seem unable to elicit a response in any other way. It is also a sign of one who seeks to exercise some form of control over the lives of others.

History has also revealed that all the major evangelists who have stood the test of time and withstood intense scrutiny share one thing in common: the preaching of the cross of Christ. The simple gospel message brings a larger response than any preaching of eternal retribution designed to generate emotions such as fear or anxiety. John Wesley, one of the most successful and well-known evangelists in history, wrote in his *Journal*, "I will never believe them to obey from fear who are dead to the motives of love." [1] Furthermore, Martin Lloyd Jones' extensive study of the evangelical Great Awakening in England concluded:

John Wesley was a man who applied no kind of [emotional] technique in his ministry; and this is equally true of George Whitefield and the other great men whom God raised up in the eighteenth century to carry through a mighty work. To suggest the contrary is to import something that is quite alien to the whole atmosphere and spirit of the great movement in the history of the church. 2

Thousands of people have had some form of emotional experience that they refer to as conversion but have never been truly converted to Christ. Conversely, thousands of people (as the testimonies of converts from Graham's crusades demonstrate) have experienced an authentic Christian conversion but felt little or no emotion at the time. They simply responded to the message by committing their lives to Christ and surrendering their wills to him. Such surrender will certainly create a revolutionary change in a convert's life, but the change is in no way based upon emotion.

In Billy Graham crusades any emotional appeal is conspicuous only because of its absence. In the meeting itself and in the counseling that follows, the appeal is based upon the elementary truth of the gospel. Impartial observers, critical journalists, and supporters of Graham have all noted the lack of emphasis upon the emotions in the campaigns. For example, Professor McKenzie, of Edinburgh University in Scotland, commented, "Apart from television, I heard Dr. Graham just once. That was in the McEwan Hall when he spoke to the principal, professors, lecturers, and students of the university. It was one of the finest cultured, evangelical addresses I have ever heard."

Likewise, a journalist for the Glasgow *Evening Citizen* wrote, "I found the atmosphere of Harringay entirely reverent and devoid of the type of things to work up the emotions which are so often associated with American evangelists." The Most Reverend Geoffrey Fisher, who personally attended Graham's London crusade, wrote in the *Canterbury Diocesan Notes*, "There was in the campaign a deliberate intention not to exploit the situation unworthily to rouse emotion; there was no revivalism." Of the Harringay Crusade he said, "Any suggestion that there was emotionalism . . . is indignantly repudiated." And as we have previously noted, Jewish columnist Herbert Weiner was surprised, while on assignment at the New York campaign, to observe "the calm, uncharged atmosphere of the crusade."

That colorful and exciting conversions do take place in the Graham crusades cannot be denied. Nor can it be denied that differences in personality and temperament produce varying degrees of intensity in response to the gospel. Emotional reactions are rooted in one's personality type and psychological disposition. Some respondents have experienced powerful, emotional decisions for Christ, while others have felt a minimum of emotion, recognizing only that they were drawn to make a decision.

Despite these differences, critics have been regularly confounded by a common discovery: Although persons of certain temperaments have been found to be particularly vulnerable to non-evangelical "conversion" experiences, such is not the case when the Holy Spirit begins the work of regeneration. The universality of the work of the Spirit is rooted in humankind's inherent need for salvation. Individuals of every temperament and background, as we shall see, respond to the invitation in similar ways and evince the same effects in their lives.

A questionnaire issued in 1957 to a random sampling of 1,000 inquirers reveals some interesting data regarding emotionalism in their conversion experience. Pertinent questions and their answers follow. (It should be noted that not all respondents answered all questions. Therefore, the numbers may not necessarily add up to 1,000-the total number of respondents.)

1. What was your emotional experience? That is, did you experience sorrow, guilt, joy, shame, fear, or any other emotion?
   a. Sorrow, guilt, or shame, followed by peace and joy   608
   b. Joy and peace   64
   c. Fear followed by peace   87

2. Was your emotional experience violent, mild, or completely lacking?
   a. Violent (or strong)   118
   b. Mild   504
   c. Completely lacking   129

3. If you experienced conversion as a crisis, how clearly can you remember the actual crisis?
   a. Very clearly   390
   b. Not very clearly   276
   c. There was no crisis   89

4. If your conversion was more gradual, do you define any particular moment as the time of the decision?
   a. Yes   129
   b. No   111

5. After the experience of your conversion, what were the remaining effects (moral change, joy and peace, release)?
   a. Moral change   189
   b. Joy and peace   365
   c. No moral change but a sense of spiritual
      satisfaction   178
   d. Release   129

The variety of responses indicated by these questionnaire results nevertheless reflect a revealing pattern: Intense emotions play an incidental role in the majority of conversions. The results also reveal certain individual differences among the respondents which support what Graham himself has to say in his *How to Be Born Again*:

> The . . . degree of emotion involved in the process which leads to our conversion is also varied. Some, but not all, will face an emotional crisis with symptoms similar to those accompanying mental conflict. They may experience deep feelings and even tears of repentance. The Holy Spirit is convicting them of sin. This is their way of responding to Him. Each of us may have a different emotional experience. The night I came to Christ there were several people around me weeping. I had no tears at all and wondered if my act of commitment was genuine.
>
> I have learned since that many have had a much quieter conversion, with a shorter time in the process. Perhaps one person, reading the Scripture or singing a hymn, comes upon a simple statement and applies it to himself then and there. Another person hears a sermon and with no stress or conflict receives its message and believes in Christ. Conversion is no less real to these quiet people than to the more expressive or dramatic ones. [3]

At one major Billy Graham crusade a most unusual conversion story was reported: A man attended ninety-nine consecutive services, finally coming forward to receive Christ on the last evening of the crusade!

In his discussion of conversion Graham goes on to detail two contrasting experiences from the New Testament. In Acts 16 Paul describes the conversion of Lydia, a seller of purple, in the city of Philippi. Hearing Paul preach one day at the side of a river, she quietly responded to his message without any emotional upheaval. The jailer Paul speaks of, however, experienced a more dramatic, turbulent conversion. As a result of an earthquake, he feared that his prisoners would escape, so he prepared to fall on his sword to escape any retribution from the authorities. Suddenly he heard the apostle Paul say to him, "Do thyself no harm: for we are all here."[4] Trembling and astonished, the jailer fell down, crying, "What must I do to be saved?" "Believe on the Lord Jesus Christ, and thou shalt be saved,"[5] responded Paul.

Graham continues:

> Jesus described the conversion experience like the movement of the wind. "The wind blows where it wishes and you hear the sound of it, but do not know where it comes from and where it is going; so is every one who is born of the Spirit" (John 3:8).
>
> Wind can be quiet, gentle, or it can reach cyclone proportions. So it is with conversion, sometimes easy and tender, and other times a tornado which alters the entire landscape.[6]

Psychological Perspectives on Emotion in Conversion

As we have noted, at the moment of the conversion crisis there is generally a surrender to whatever the individual conceives to be a higher power. That power may be thought of as nothing more than the vague "determiner of destiny." Although this definition of deity is not completely satisfactory to those enlightened by the Spirit of God, nevertheless the experience may be a genuine, though not an evangelical, religious crisis. In other words, it is entirely possible that a crisis of a religious nature may be induced through emotional stimuli unrelated to the gospel message.

Some persons, of course, never go beyond the mild stimulus that satisfied the aesthetic sensibility. Such individuals may find their religious desire satisfied by viewing a beautiful stained-glass window or hearing a majestic piece by Bach played on a fine pipe organ. The roots of religion are numerous, and the response of the individual will vary with temperament and training.

Psychologist George A. Coe, author of *The Spiritual Life*,[7] posited that there are four basic emotional types of personality. These types roughly correspond to the traditional classifications of *sanguine* (cheerful and optimistic), *melancholic* (sad and depressed), *choleric* (hot-tempered, easily angered), and *phlegmatic* (stolid, impassive). When these varying emotional dispositions are considered in combination with environmental multiplicities, we can easily understand how many complex factors enter into a conversion experience.

Historical research, as well as scrutiny of hundreds of testimonies, reveals another convenient way of categorizing conversion experience, consisting of three different primary orientations: the emotional stimulus response, the intellectual response, and the moral response.

The Emotional Stimulus Type

From a psychological point of view, the emotional type of conversion is that in which one falls in love with an ideal. In many respects this falling in love may resemble *sensual* love, and certainly that adjective may describe the tone of a number of religious meetings. Medieval mystics frequently found such an orientation suitable to their personality and to their times. The conversion of Francis of Assisi, for example, may be characterized as a falling in love with Christ. Many of the Sufi poets had experiences similar to that of St. Francis. One such poet wrote the following:

> Love thrilled the chord of my soul's lute,
> And changed me all to love from head to foot,
> 'Twas but a moment's touch, yet shall Time ever
> To me the debt of thanksgiving impute. [8]

In their use of the language of human love to express their affection for the Divine Lover, many of the medieval mystics resemble the Sufis and Hindu bhaktas. When St. Francis plighted his troth to Christ, for example, he satisfied all the romantic aspirations of a soul filled with the medieval ideals of chivalry.

Underwood, who included in his study many stories from India, described the characteristics of many Indian conversions in this way:

> The conversion of most, if not all of the bhakti saints of India, was a falling in love with the deity on whom they lavished their devotion. Chaitanya's love for Krishna amounted to a passion. Sometimes he would imagine he was Radha, Krishna's mistress. "I make my heart imagine her emotions," he said, "and thus I taste the delicious sweetness of Krishna." [9]

The orders of sisters in the Roman Catholic communion find a satisfaction comparable to that of human love when they accept the marriage ring as a token of becoming the bride of Christ. Other examples of emotional relationships with Christ have occurred throughout the history of Christianity. For example, the wife of Jonathan Edwards wrote a particularly moving account of such an experience:

> [It was] the sweetest night I ever had in my life. I never before, for so long a time together, enjoyed so much of the light and rest and sweetness of heaven in my soul, but without the least agitation of body during the whole time. Part of the night I lay awake, sometimes asleep, and sometimes between sleeping and waking. But all night I continued in a constant, clear, and lovely sense of the heavenly sweetness of Christ's excellent love, of his nearness to me, and of my dearness to him, with an inexpressibly sweet calmness of soul in an entire rest in him. [10]

The caution that must be applied to the emotional stimulus type of experience is that pure emotion may not be substituted for a response to the content of the gospel and a commitment of the will to the Person of Christ.

The Intellectual Type

This type of orientation may be found in any religious persuasion—Christian or non-Christian. St. Augustine is a Christian example of one whose confession of faith places him in the intellectual category. As the result of an intense interior struggle, Augustine, upon hearing a voice say, "Take up and read," opened the Bible to Romans 13. There he read the words, "Let us walk honestly, as in the day; not in rioting and drunkenness, not in chambering and wantonness, not in strife and envying. But put ye on the Lord Jesus Christ, and make not provison for the flesh, to fulfil the lusts thereof."[11] As a result of reading this Scripture passage, Augustine found the peace he had been looking for.

A particularly apt example of an intellectually oriented conversion is that of Charles G. Finney (1792-1875). He described his experience in his *Memoirs*:

> In studying elementary law, I found the old authors frequently quoting the Scriptures. . . . This excited my curiosity so much that I went and purchased a Bible. . . . I read and meditated on it much more than I had ever done before in my life. . . . But as I read my Bible . . . I became very restless. . . . It seemed to me that there must be something in religion that was of infinite importance; and it was soon settled with me, that if the soul was immortal, I needed a great change in my inward state to be prepared for the happiness of heaven. But still my mind was not made up as to the truth or falsehood of the gospel and the Christian religion. The question, however, was of too much importance to allow me to rest in any uncertainty on the subject. . . . This being settled, I was brought face to face with the question whether I would accept Christ as presented in the gospel or pursue a worldly course of life. At this period, my mind, as I have since known, was so much impressed by the Holy Spirit, that I could not long leave this question unsettled; nor could I long hesitate between two courses of life presented to me. . . . On a Sabbath evening in the autumn of 1821, I made up my mind that I would settle the question of my soul's salvation at once. . . . The whole question of gospel salvation opened up to me in a manner most marvelous to me at the time. I think then I saw as clearly as I ever have in my life, the reality and fullness of the atonement of Christ.[12]

Psychologists have long recognized that learning occurs in levels and that peaks of learning are reached, not gradually, but by sudden bursts of intellectual insight. By analogy it may be said that spiritual knowledge also is arrived at by such bursts, but that intellectual energy left to itself is never sufficient to raise the natural mind above natural levels.

The searching individual must find a solution to his problems, and such a solution can lead to the crisis of commitment to Christ in faith. Although the way of the emotional stimulus type is simpler than that of intellectuals, their perils are not fewer, for they are in danger of experiencing a crisis that is merely humanistic.

Today's humanist often understands the significance and importance of having religious values in one's life. Christian faith is cognitive, meaningful, grounded in history, and rational in the sense that it rests on firm grounds of belief that will withstand the most exacting scrutiny and investigation.

The Moral Type

Although Underwood included this type in his classification, it does not have as many distinguishing characteristics as the other types we have discussed. One example of a moral orientation in conversion is that of Adoniram Judson. The stimulus for his crisis experience was his confrontation with his intellectual pride, which resulted from his phenomenal achievements at college. It was the growth of this pride that brought Judson to consider his own need of salvation.

An example of moral change effected by a religious orientation is that of Alcoholics Anonymous (A A). The organization's implied belief in God (as Higher Power) is the basis of one's being "saved" from alcoholism. Despite the tremendously edifying results of A A programs, the moral change experienced by alcoholics is not identical to that of Christian conversion, based as it is on a commitment to the *Person* of Christ.

Another similarity, however, between the deliverance from alcohol experienced in A A and the deliverance from sin experienced in Christian conversion is found in the experience of *grace*. Both experiences result from the recognition that one is personally unable to straighten out his own life. It is only in one's admission of inability, not in the boast of strength, that one finds deliverance. It is through surrender that strength comes.

Emotion and Testimonies

To conclude this survey of the role of emotion in conversion, let us take a look at several testimonies of converts in Graham's crusades. These stories vary in the degree to which emotion was present during the crisis experience.

I met a friend who asked me to join him and go to hear Billy Graham. Already I knew about him, for there had been wide publicity in Manila. I was impressed when I saw how many had come to hear him, and I wondered if all these people were Protestants. I found out that many of them were just like me. They were curious and hungry. Then when the choir started to sing, I felt that they had a joy I didn't have, but I wanted it. Then Billy preached. I thought he would tell about America, or his travels, or something about the political conditions in the world. He didn't talk about them at all. He began telling us what the Bible said. He didn't stop, but kept on giving verses from the Bible.

I remember how he told of the man who got rich, and had so many goods that he tore down his barns to build greater ones. Then the Lord said something about, "What does it profit a man if he gain the whole world but lose his own soul?" While Billy Graham was preaching, I was quiet, just thinking about the meaning of this Scripture. I didn't think about doing anything more. That is why I was so surprised when he gave the invitation. I didn't know anything about going forward or deciding. I always thought that we had to earn salvation by doing things; and the more we do the better our chances are.

That is why I was taken by surprise. He asked me to receive something. I felt that I wasn't good enough, and right while I was thinking that way, he said something about coming just as you are. Without giving it much more thought, I got up and went forward.

From this relatively uneventful, unemotional conversion, we move to a more dramatic one:

We came upon the huge place where the crowd was gathering, and we went in. I'll never forget how I felt. I wondered what to expect that could cause such a crowd to come to hear him.

The meeting got under way, and it seemed very short. In thirty minutes it was over, or at least I thought so. Then my friend explained to me that this had been only "The Hour of Decision" broadcast. I was glad that there was going to be more. In spite of my wicked life, I had a desire to know God and to have peace in my own soul.

When the regular service began, Billy Graham changed his style. He had been preaching . . . about world affairs and their meaning. Now he began to search *my* soul. His preaching was so direct that I couldn't miss its meaning. . . . I held onto my seat while Billy gave the invitation. I can't explain why, but I did. I said to myself I wouldn't go, even though it was what I knew I should do. I was having a terrific battle that only the Lord and I knew anything about. Billy had closed the invitation, and I still sat there. Suddenly I wasn't able to resist any longer. I felt as if the earth would swallow me up. Something pulled me out of my seat, and then I actually ran to where the people were standing.

And finally, a New York homemaker tells her story:

I cannot forget that night. As Billy preached, I cried. I knew in my heart that this was the right thing to do. I remember he said, "Just believe it now," and it all seemed so simple, too simple to save anyone. He talked about the witness of the Spirit, and I hadn't the faintest idea what that meant.

As Billy finally gave the invitation, I thought he should ask some hard thing for us to do. I just couldn't think that salvation was a gift. I remember I spoke to my sister and asked her if all I had to do was to go forward. She said it was; it's so simple. . . . It was what I had always wanted, so I went forward. A wonderful woman helped me when I came to the counseling room, but I was too preoccupied to pay much attention. But as I looked at the verses she showed me, I remembered my whole life and knew I needed forgiveness for many sins. I wept when I thought how much Christ loved me to die for me, and I still weep when I think of it. I cannot understand how he should have cared for me, but I know he did. It's just like the Bible says. I was so relieved and happy when I had finally come to Christ and he had accepted me.

Chapter Five

How Lives Are Changed: Testimonies From Around the World

Surely the primary measure of the effectiveness of public evangelism is that of actual results in individual lives. Our Lord himself gave us the criterion when he said, "By their fruits ye shall know them." All other considerations aside—and they are far from insignificant—the first question to be asked is always this: "What really happened to those who professed conversion?" [1]

Thus Frank E. Gaebelein, in his introduction to my 1958 book, *Persuaded to Live*, expresses the importance of knowing the individual testimonies of converts in Graham crusades. Literally thousands of people from all walks of life, all socioeconomic groups, all professions, all age groups, all nationalities, all religious persuasions, and all political affiliations have recorded their testimonies for perusal by anyone who is interested.

Before looking at a sampling of the thrilling conversion stories told by individuals the world around, we may ask what lessons can be learned from reading these testimonies.

First, they demonstrate how few people have realized what it means to be a Christian. One convert, for example, wrote, "I was reared in the church and have always been active in church work. Naturally I assumed that I was a Christian." A young woman indicated that she had felt she was a Christian because she was not a Hindu, Muslim, or a member of some other religious tradition. A senior citizen said, "I thought I was a Christian because I had always tried to live the best life possible, and I thought God would somehow overlook my mistakes because I had tried."

Each of these testimonies reveals ignorance of what it means to be a Christian. Christianity is not primarily a system of ethics, nor is it merely an affiliation with some religious organization.

Billy Graham has often said to his crusade audiences, "You came into this meeting not thinking that you could leave a new person, but you can be a new person before you go out."

The second lesson we can learn from conversion stories is that, although there are many preliminary factors, the new birth takes place at a specific, locatable time, often suddenly and frequently without warning. Many observers who think the conversion phenomenon can be fully understood intellectually are inclined to deny the possibility of dramatic, immediate transformations. The testimonies gathered here testify to the genuineness of dramatic conversion.

The third truth illustrated by the conversion stories is: "If any man be in Christ, he is a new creature: old things are passed away; behold, all things are become new."[2]   Testimony after testimony bears witness to the newness of life felt as a result of conversion. A skid row alcoholic of thirty years suddenly became a sober man. A burdened, discouraged, handicapped person discovered a grace that gave him a new reason for living. A proud, selfish husband became humble and compassionate. And the stories go on and on.

Fourth, we discover from the experiences of the converts that the new birth has no natural explanation. Rather, the transforming crisis in the life of an individual is best explained in supra-human terms. It is "the power of God unto salvation to every one that believeth."[3]   Only such a power can work the revolutionary changes we will read about in this chapter.

That there is no human being existing who is beyond hope is the next lesson of conversion. Jesus said, "I am not come to call the righteous, but sinners to repentance." Whether they were socially well-adjusted, successful individuals, or social outcasts—alcoholics, drug addicts, and economically deprived persons—converts tell the same story of responding to a message that generated new hope for their lives. They suddenly realized that they were loved—the greatest need of a human being. The final message illustrated in the conversion accounts is that the gospel is still the power of God for salvation to "every one that believeth."[4]

Napoleon once said, "Alexander the Great, Caesar, and I have founded great empires upon force. Today our empires are crumbled. Jesus Christ founded a kingdom based upon love, and today there are millions who would die for him." The modern-day miracle of conversion to Jesus Christ confirms the faith and hope of believers everywhere. The gospel contradicts the world and is in opposition to it. Yet its attraction is felt in every generation by men and women of every race. Its magnetism is in no way diminished by the technological and scientific advances of our day. It was St. Augustine who said, "Thou hast formed us for thyself and our soul is restless until it rests in thee."

One of the most poignant conversion stories recorded is that of Matsuyo, the daughter of a Buddhist priest in Tokyo. Deeply and desperately unhappy for most of her life, she had begun to pray daily that she might find some kind of peace with God. As day after day passed with no apparent answer to her prayer, she became angry and frustrated.

One day, however, Matsuyo went to visit a good friend who was dying. As she stepped into the friend's room, she saw written over the bed the words, "I am the Way, the Truth, and the Life." Although she didn't fully comprehend these words and had no idea that they were from the Bible, she thought perhaps this verse might have something to do with her persistent prayers.

Upon leaving her friend's home, Matsuyo met a Japanese pastor who handed her a ticket, telling her to go to the Tokyo stadium to hear Billy Graham in a one-day rally. On the ticket were printed the words she had just seen in her friend's home: "I am the Way, the Truth, and the Life."

Arriving at the stadium at the rally's scheduled time, Matsuyo was bitterly disappointed to find the stadium full to capacity. The police guarding the gate would allow no additional persons to enter. Matsuyo walked up to one of the policemen, begging him to let her in so she could stand in the back. Responding that he had no right to allow her in, the officer nevertheless turned his back to her and engaged someone else in conversation, allowing her to enter. Although there was standing room only inside the stadium, Matsuyo did get to hear Graham's message. And then for the third time, she saw the words, "I am the Way, the Truth, and the Life" written on the banner hanging over the platform. Fearful of being too exuberant too soon, Matsuyo nevertheless responded to Graham's invitation in the overcrowded stadium. He simply asked all those who wished to receive Jesus as Savior to raise their hands and then to write their name and address on a slip of paper and hand it to an usher as they left the stadium.

Having turned in her slip of paper, Matsuyo made her way home, continuing to pray steadfastly. Eventually growing discouraged, she felt that even Graham had let her down by not responding to her name and address. Within three weeks, however, Matsuyo received in the mail Graham's book *Peace With God*, translated into Japanese. And it was through this little volume that Matsuyo finally found peace with God. Her sparkling witness and peaceful air testified to the transformation that she had experienced.

From the other side of the globe comes the testimony of a convert in Billy Graham's first London crusade. A Member of Parliament (M.P.) and a leading industrialist in Britain, this man has, since his conversion, become well acquainted with members of Graham's team. When asked if he had been a Christian before becoming an inquirer at the crusade, this Briton said, "I was thoroughly Orthodox, although I never read the Bible. I assumed I was a Christian on Orthodox principle."

Continuing to describe his spiritual journey, the M.P. revealed numerous problems that had plagued him over the years. A severe illness and a serious sports injury both had caused him to come face to face with his mortality. He had been unable to keep a number of resolutions he had made in good faith. One day he received a call from his brother-in-law, who had been converted in one of Graham's Swiss crusades. Full of glowing reports, the brother-in-law urged the M.P. to attend the London crusade. Agreeing to promote and attend the campaign, the man eventually found himself having a conversation with Graham himself. He later recalled, "Billy told me I was an outsider. I didn't know his unmovable loyalty to the Scriptures."

This brief conversation sent this prominent Britisher on a search for a personal Savior, whom he came to know shortly afterward. "Billy Graham's continual emphasis, 'The Bible says,'

. . . gave me a sense of guilt. I became desperately miserable. . . . I felt I had wasted a lot of time in this life. . . ." As a result of his dramatic transformation, this man became a church warden, organized effective children's services, became a counselor, and helped in the business affairs of the church.

John, a college student, wrote his testimony:

> I had read much of the Bible and had attended church, but the church in which I grew up never, to my memory, ever stated that one had to submit personally to Christ and could henceforth have a personal relationship with him. Looking back, my salvation experience was quite a *revolutionary idea*. I'd led a moral life. I felt comfortable in the church, but not so around people who spoke of a personal relationship with Jesus Christ, and least of all in the presence of Billy Graham's media presentation; yet something inside told me to listen. When I heard the message one night, I realized I had no assurance of any real satisfaction in being moral or religious. In short, I saw its phoniness and worthlessness before the Holy Almighty Judge. I decided to stop running from God, to run instead for God and to run to him. I hope I can someday help others to do the same."

Numerous unsolicited letters reveal the duration of many converts' conversion experiences. One woman from Memphis wrote to Graham:

> As the years go by, I am more and more thankful and grateful for our gracious Lord. Many times I have recalled the day God sent you to this city to preach the gospel of the Lord Jesus Christ. Jesus reached down in his mercy and washed a young girl of fourteen years of age in his blood. I will never forget that, though I forget everything else."

Another expression of gratitude came from a convert in Tygh Valley, Oregon: "It has been ten years in August since I was saved in your campaign. I want to let you know I am still walking with the Lord." Such letters are the source of great inspiration to the Graham team, who have carried on the work of evangelizing the world for more than forty years.

Some of the individuals who came to Christ in the crusades had been intensely religious most of their lives. One such woman wrote when she was seventy years old: "My life was a 'Christian type' of life. It was happy because I had a good family background. I went to church, was baptized as a baby, and confirmed. Later I went to Sunday school and also taught and had many loving friends and relatives. I married a 'Christian type' man and worked hard at bringing up a 'Christian type' daughter." Such a testimony shows how possible it is to be close to being a Christian without having actually made a personal commitment to Christ.

Crini was one of the converts who came to Christ in the Graham crusade in Calcutta. A manager in the Indian Overseas Bank, Crini was the son of Hindu parents. As a child he had attended a Christian school in Madras for a time, had seen slides of the life of Christ, and had even studied the Bible. He believed that Christ was a great social reformer, but nothing more.

While attending university, Crini was influenced to become an atheist and subsequently became critical of the Bible. Realizing he had no faith, he turned to a series of ideologies, but found no interior satisfaction. Filling his life with worldly pursuits, Crini eventually found himself with psychological problems and at odds with his family. One day Crini, by now a bank officer, found out that his secretary was singing in the choir for the Billy Graham crusade in Calcutta. Because of her competence and integrity, he agreed to attend the crusade, where Graham preached upon the text, "I am the way, the truth, and the life: no man cometh unto the Father, but by me."[5]   The power of this text went straight to Crini's heart and mind, and he realized he was without God in this world.

It is Crini's testimony that Graham's use of the Bible convinced him of his need for Christ. He was also deeply touched by Jesus' words on the cross: "Father, forgive them; for they know not what they do."[6]   He had never encountered such compassion in his voracious reading, his experimentation with diverse ideologies, and his successful professional life. In reflecting on his conversion, Crini said, "The fullness of your talents never comes to life until you surrender to Christ. I had talents but could not use them fully."

One unusual testimony comes from a man born to Jewish parents in Vienna, Austria, in 1937. As a result of the Holocaust, he emigrated to the United States in 1939. He writes that after his emigration:

[I] did not continue to be brought up in a truly Jewish, religiously Jewish, home. A number of people planted seeds along the way, until I reached high school, where I met a friend who witnessed to me and then attended with my dad and me the St. Louis Billy Graham crusade. Subsequently both my parents and I received Christ. After graduation from college, I attended seminary and then entered the Christian ministry. My continuing concern for people led me into a special kind of ministry.

Although the external circumstances of converts in foreign countries may differ from those closer to home, there is, nevertheless, a common thread running through all the testimonies. Esene Ikon, a young man living in the heart of Nigeria, with no knowledge of God, was planning to be a juju priest. One day as he was walking along a path in the African bush, he saw a tract lying in front of him. As a result of reading the tract and encountering John 3:16: "For God so loved the world, that he gave his only begotten Son, that whosoever believeth in him should not perish, but have everlasting life," Esene began to attend a church and read the Bible. He dates his conversion experience from the day he first encountered the Christian message in the tract that "accidentally" lay in his path.

Another convert from the other side of the globe is an insurance worker from Madras, who has taken the Christian name of Paul. One day as Paul was at work, an acquaintance came to tell him that the American evangelist Billy Graham was going to be speaking and he wanted to invite Paul to attend. Unaware of the meaning of the word *evangelist*, Paul decided to go hear this American speaker. Fascinated with Graham's message, Paul returned for four more successive crusade meetings. Taking an observer stance each night, sitting in the last row of seats, he discovered an unaccustomed joy and peace pervading his being while listening to the gospel message. Finally, on the fifth night of the crusade, Paul went forward to receive Christ as his Savior. Although he later said that he had not felt the need to go forward to be assured of salvation, he nevertheless thought he ought to make his confession public.

As a former Hindu, Paul encountered resistance to his conversion from his family. Despite their rejection, Paul persevered in his newfound faith, eventually preparing himself for the Christian ministry. He had a burning desire to share the gospel with his own people. Paul is still active in evangelistic work in his native India.

One of the most detailed conversion stories is that of Barbara, a young woman who made her decision for Christ alone in her apartment late one night. She tells about her friend Eddie, who had been converted in the crusade in Madison Square Garden in 1957. Eddie had witnessed to Barbara, asking her to attend the crusade with him. Joining him at the rally, Barbara heard for the first time the message of Christ dying for her sins. Although she did not go forward at the crusade, Barbara remembered the message she had heard. After a year of setbacks and problems, Barbara finally gave her life to Christ. She writes:

> My need for God and salvation was apparent throughout my last year of struggle, from the time at Graham's meetings when I first heard of Christ dying for my sins until I was converted. Double pneumonia, a personal tragedy that nearly cost me my life, and business failures hastened my decision. . . . I had attended the Graham crusade with my friend Eddie because I was curious and I wondered what religious people thought. I had dabbled a little with spiritualism for amusement, and I thought, I guess, that attending a revival would round out my education. I heard Billy Graham preach three times on the Ten Commandments, and then I refused to attend with Eddie anymore because I contended that the crusade was a fake. Actually, I was in utter terror because I thought God would pick me up out of my seat, send me forward to be converted, and make a fool out of me in front of all those people.

Reporting that she had come from a broken home marked by bitter fighting, Barbara had left home at nineteen, "determined never to be dependent on anyone but myself again, or to expose myself to the possibility of being hurt." She eventually became an actress and company manager of a children's theater troupe touring the United States. She subsequently settled in New York where she modeled, acted in off-broadway productions and on television, danced, exhibited her oil paintings, wrote plays, and worked as a comedienne. A highly creative perfectionist, Barbara found herself subject to guilt, depression, and uncontrolled temper tantrums. Feeling possessed by a fierce power over which she had no control, Barbara felt hopeless about her life. Eventually she realized her own inability to secure peace and happiness. As a later result of Graham's preaching, Barbara began to attend a Christian group where she heard the Bible expounded. She says:

> One night I went home [from the Bible study], thoroughly disgusted with myself, recognizing the shallowness and illogical nature of my arguments. [I discovered] that I had no reasonable explanation for not believing in Christ as my Lord and Savior. Alone that night, I cried and asked, "Why can't I believe? What is keeping me from God?" And then it seemed that I heard the Lord for the first time telling me what I know he must have been saying all along, only I had turned a deaf ear to his voice. I heard his quiet voice speaking to me firmly but gently. In a split second I knew that pride was my great sin, and that I was now faced with making a decision for or against Christ. That night I brokenly asked God to help me acknowledge Christ. My temper vanished completely, along with my guilt, fears, anxieties, tensions, prejudices, and inhibitions. Losing myself in Christ, I no longer avoided people as I had done off-stage. I had a message which I had to share, and which gave me a fearlessness to talk to people who would have seemed quite unapproachable before. I no longer felt the necessity to lie and to cover up my life. The Son of God had covered my sins, blotted them out forever, and I was no longer ashamed to admit that I was not perfect. For the first time I felt the ability to forgive others and to understand and love those whom I had shunned before. My relationship with my parents, never close or friendly, was restored to peaceful affection. To my amazement and constant gratitude, my aversion to marriage was lessened through God's help and . . . the Lord brought great joy into my life when I took my marriage vows to my husband, a former actor now preparing for the Christian ministry.

New Delhi, India, was the home of Elisha, the son of a Presbyterian pastor. Although Elisha considered himself a Christian, he never studied the Bible and had never made a decision concerning salvation. One day Elisha read in the local papers that Billy Graham was conducting a crusade. Full of curiosity, Elisha decided to attend a rally. Although Graham's message reiterated much that Elisha had heard before, somehow this time he *perceived* the gospel message in a new way. As the invitation was given to come forward, Elisha made his way to the front of the auditorium. "I knew something had happened, but I didn't know what it was," Elisha said. With the encouragement of family and friends, Elisha grew in his spiritual life and eventually prepared for the Christian ministry. Today he is serving God among his people in India.

A Pennsylvania woman with all the material blessings of life tells her story:

Before giving my life to Jesus, I attended a church but had little faith. I was distant from God. I had never even heard of a personal relationship with Jesus. I was constantly worried about coming down with some serious illness. I was terrified of death. I was a revengeful person, and most of all I was unhappy. Even though my husband has a successful business and we own a Lincoln Continental and a beautiful, new, luxurious home, all the material things by which the world measures happiness, I was so very unhappy. I couldn't sleep without a tranquilizer. . . . Mentally tortured day and night, I reached out to God. . . . I was watching Billy Graham on television. His magnetic power in speaking God's Word was what I so desperately needed to hear. I realized I could have a personal relationship with God which I had never known was possible. My life was at an all-time low. . . . After surrendering my life to Jesus, I began to change. I hungered to read the Bible, I prayed each day and made Jesus Lord of my life. I am no longer concerned about dying. I don't need pills to sleep because I have peace and joy. My life has never been happier because I do not walk alone.

Wayne was a young University of Minnesota student who described his life this way: "My life was empty. I guess I'd have to say that I was my own god. That is, I was running my own life. . . . But as a result of certain individuals and circumstances in my life, the Holy Spirit began to create within me an interest in the Word of God and in the church." Eventually invited to attend the Billy Graham meetings at the Minnesota State Fairgrounds, Wayne accepted Christ and went to the follow-up meetings for inquirers at the First Covenant church.

"I later became a member of that church," reports Wayne. "My life changed quite radically. . . . I got involved in Campus Crusade for Christ. I became a Sunday school officer. I offered my life fully to Christ and sought to know from the Lord what I could do with the rest of my life, how I could best invest it for him, to bring him the greatest glory." The answer to Wayne's prayer came, and he enrolled in Bethel Theological Seminary and eventually became a Baptist pastor, ministering in California.

One aspect of Graham's ministry that has been the means of opening up people to the gospel is his television and radio outreach. One person who first listened to Graham on radio was Pat, a young man from the Minneapolis area. Although Pat recalled that as a child he had had considerable Bible teaching from his mother as well as from his church, he had strayed far from the Word of God. He recounts his story: "I had just about reached the end of my rope. I was unemployed; I was separated from my wife; I had been drinking more than I should; I had failed in everything I had attempted. I had the feeling that this [Graham's Minneapolis crusade] was my last chance. If I didn't commit myself to Jesus Christ now, I never would. I felt that I was doomed if I didn't make my decision then." Responding to the invitation at the rally, Pat went forward with hundreds of people streaming down the aisles.

Although at the time Pat had no way of knowing the effect his decision would have on his life, he said, some years later: "The Holy Spirit came into my heart, and I have a peace and assurance of salvation. . . . It seems quite likely that we [his wife and he] are going to settle our differences and remake our home. This is just one of the many other blessings too numerous to mention here."

The Manila crusade saw a young Filipino named Benjamin in attendance. Drawn to the meetings because he had heard that Billy Graham was a great preacher, Benjamin hoped that he might find some help for his spiritual problems. Recalling his conversion experience, he noted that the passage from the Word of God that made an impact him was: "As many as received him, to them gave he power to become the sons of God."[7] Today Benjamin's life is dedicated to Christian service.

Roger was a watchman in a factory in New Brunswick. He had first read about Billy Graham in a *Reader's Digest* article. Finding that some of his acquaintances were going to attend a Billy Graham meeting, Roger decided to join the group. He tells his story:

> I was brought up to do good, not ever to steal, cheat, lie, hate, covet, lust, and so on. . . . But in spite of my parents' fine example and a religious upbringing, these ways were a part of my life. From the time of my youth I had wanted to be a professional hockey player. I thought no sacrifice was too great to reach that goal. However, as time passed and I realized I would never achieve my dream, I began to feel aimless, empty, and hopeless. I had been in and out of three universities seeking truth and fulfillment, but only in the power of Jesus Christ could my desperate search end. . . . [As a result of the crusade] I was immediately inspired to live for Jesus. My desire for things I formerly coveted seemed to vanish and he enabled me to find joy in him and gave me assurance of salvation and forgiveness. I was conscious of changes and sometimes I didn't understand what was going on in my life, but I knew that God had his hand on my life and he still does, and I am grateful at this moment. I have failed him many times, and sometimes terribly, but I am realizing the power of his Word and the influence of the Holy Spirit and prayer. I look forward to greater stability in my walk with God as I continue with him.

A heavy equipment operator named John described his life this way in his testimony:

> I was lost, bitter, hurt, afraid, sad, lonely, mentally and spiritually hungry, tired, ashamed, just like a brick house that has burned down. The walls stand, but there's nothing inside. There are no words to describe this hell I was living in with myself. Yet I had to keep up a front in the business world every day. . . . It all began on television. I had followed Dr. Graham in every way I could for about three years. Although I was preparing to make a decision, I waited for Dr. Graham to come to Indianapolis before I actually went through with the decision. . . . [My life feels] as if a door opened and it was heartbreaking to realize that I had waited so long to open it. My whole conception of life, people, friends, church, work, human relations, and everything in general has changed.

A musician who found Christ gives his testimony:

> As a youth I became interested in the trumpet and spent tremendous amounts of time studying classical music. My life was isolationist, introverted, and intellectually oriented. Loneliness pervaded my life. Though I believed in the supernatural reality of Jesus, I never grew spiritually from a simple salvation experience, although God miraculously allowed me to go to Northwestern University and to study music.
>
> I had no way of dealing with the secular reasoning of the intellectual community. I had a four-year-old's concept of Christianity, while dealing with adult humanistic philosophies and dogmas. I got into drugs, rock music, and radical literature. Although I met some Christian friends in school, I gravitated more and more toward the lifestyle of a dropout. As a junior, burned out and confused, I left school. I was at a dead end, searching for meaning.

As a result of his subsequent conversion, this young man began to sense the reality of God's presence in his life, but he was also aware of the power of Satan as a real force. "I sensed his attacks and attempts to undermine my faith in God. I was Satan's newly lost toy, and he was throwing a temper tantrum." As this convert became increasingly earnest in his desire to live for God, he began to attend church, read the Bible, pray, and otherwise cultivate his spiritual growth. Step by step he rebuilt his shattered life, mentally, socially, musically, and intellectually. He found Christian friends and grew in his ability to discern the truth. His life of isolation was replaced with one of friendship; his introversion was replaced with extroversion, his

confusion with comprehension and a sense of direction. He truly
became a "new creature in Christ."

One of the more dramatic testimonies recorded is that of a
young woman named Emma:

> At the age of seventeen, my first child was born. I was unmarried. At
> eighteen I was married, but the marriage lasted only six months. I became
> involved in drugs and prostitution and eventually ended up in a mental
> hospital. Discharged without medical permission, I shot myself and
> ended up once again in a psychiatric facility.

After being discharged a month later, Emma was told by a
doctor that she might well be on tranquilizers for the rest of her
life. By now she was the mother of three children and began to
want to set some sort of example for her two daughters and one
son. One night she turned on the television and discovered that
Billy Graham was preaching from the Old Testament. She got out
her Bible and searched for Graham's text. As a result of hearing
Graham and searching the Scriptures, Emma began to attend
church sporadically. She concludes her story by saying:

> The next time I saw a television program with Billy Graham, I telephoned
> for some counseling, and it was then that I finally received the assurance
> of my salvation. God had met my need through Graham by way of radio,
> television, and newspapers, and I thank God for him.

And our final testimony is that of a man named Richard, an
inmate at Dartmore Prison in England. He wrote to Graham:

> I have just read one of your wonderful books, *Peace With God*. I have just
> become a Christian, and the book has helped me in so many ways. . . . Life
> before was so dark and dim, but now life is bright, even here in Dartmore
> Prison. Yes, the Lord can forgive anyone for anything. I thought I would be
> the last person on earth to be forgiven for my sins. I am glad to know that I
> can do God's work even here in prison.

The remarkable universality of the gospel message produces
the equally remarkable unanimity in the global testimonies we
have read. Only the transforming power of a personal salvation
experience could have elicited the stories we have just shared.
The indelible effects of the Christian conversion experience will
reverberate in the lives of these men and women, as well as in the
lives of all those they touch for time and eternity.

Chapter Six

Nominal Christians and the Conversion Experience

One evening during the Upper Midwest Crusade in Minnesota, a young man in clerical garb responded to Graham's invitation to come forward and receive Christ. A graduate of both a Lutheran college and seminary, this young pastor had brought his youth group to hear Billy Graham, hoping to give the adolescents a religious-educational experience. Much to the pastor's initial surprise, eighteen of the twenty-five group members went forward at Graham's invitation. Beginning to reflect on his own religious history, the cleric concluded that he had never personally met Christ or committed his life to him. He, too, realized his need for personal salvation. After spending some time in prayer with one of the crusade counselors, he remarked, "In college and seminary I learned all about Jesus Christ. Tonight I met him and can now say I know him."

Stories similar to this one occur again and again throughout the testimonies received from those who have gone forward at Billy Graham crusades over the years. In a random sampling of approximately 500 questionnaires culled from the thousands of questionnaires and letters returned to the Graham team by converts, the following statistics are noteworthy. The question on the survey reads:

Before your decision to receive Christ, did you think you were a Christian?

Yes	197
No	122
Unsure	129
Nominally	28
I assumed I was	3
I didn't think about it	13

(Some of the respondents did not answer this particular question.)

It is evident from these responses that a surprisingly large number of individuals converted in the crusades had previously thought of themselves as Christians. Subsequent to their conversion experience, however, the majority of them concluded that they had not truly been Christians at all but merely nominal or cultural Christians. This perception became a turning point in the lives of many of those who had come forward. Many of these converts now describe themselves as "born-again Christians" to distinguish the quality of their present commitment to Christ from that which predated their crusade conversion.

One of the reasons many people assume that they are Christians when in fact they are only nominally so is that a number of countries and cultures in the world today have a long tradition of Christian idealism and ethics. For example, the United States, Canada, Great Britain, and Australia in particular are perceived as such "Christian" nations that it is easy to assume their citizens are automatically born Christians. The strong religious conventions that govern social customs and moral values lead people to believe that true Christianity is pervasive. It is necessary, however, to distinguish here between cultural Christianity and the experience of conversion to Christ. These two phenomena are not identical.

Numerous converts who have scrutinized their pre-existing attitudes in the light of their conversion have discovered that it was Graham's invitation to "give your life to Christ" that awakened in them doubt and uncertainty about whether they were actually Christians. It was only after hearing the gospel message that they perceived they had been living a merely *cultural* Christian life because of the context in which they had grown up. One convert said, "I thought I was a Christian, but now I know I wasn't." Such statements are, of course, much more typical of the United States and Great Britain than of non-Christian cultures like those of India, Japan, or China.

One young man typical of those who confused being "religious" with being "saved" was Paul. He wrote, "For many years I had been blinded by Satan into thinking that peace of heart could be obtained only by our own efforts." Paul had even attended a missionary college that had supported this misconception and then spent two years on the mission field on behalf of this denomination. "Although I sold Bible literature, still I was without God's grace," he said.

Then Paul met a young woman who had received Jesus as her Savior at a Billy Graham crusade in Germany. "I realized she had something that I did not possess," he stated. "At first I thought it was her strong personality, but I soon realized that One greater than she was dwelling in her." The "chance" meeting with this young woman started Paul on a search that culminated in his attendance at the Billy Graham crusade in Manchester, England. After his conversion he wrote to Graham, "I know now that by God's grace, even though we make mistakes, Christ gives us supernatural power over sin."

A typical example of cultural Christianity was one young man who expressed the sentiments of so many surveyed after crusades. When asked if he had thought he was a Christian prior to his decision, he answered, "Yes, I thought we all were." A similar response was given in Britain by the Member of Parliament cited earlier, who said that he assumed he was a Christian "on orthodox principle." Likewise, the M.P.'s wife said she had assumed she was a Christian and that she had "never heard about being reborn."

There is another group of respondents, however, who indicated they were unsure about whether they were Christians. One such man said, "There was always a doubt." Another stated, "I never felt good enough; I always did good things, was a humanitarian."

Although there were a number of Americans, as well as other Westerners, who said they had not been Christians prior to going forward at a Graham crusade, the percentage of those surveyed in non-Western cultures who gave the same answer was considerably higher. For example, nearly all those who had been converted in Hong Kong answered "no." Many of these respondents had been Buddhists or Muslims. Large numbers of converts interviewed in Japan and India also said they had not considered themselves Christians prior to going forward at a crusade. The country of India, however, reflected an unusually disparate response among converts. Nearly all converts surveyed in Delhi and Calcutta indicated that they had not been Christians before the Graham crusade, while many respondents in Madras said they had considered themselves Christians prior to crusade attendance.

Let's take a look at some more of the testimonies of converts who had thought they were Christians before their conversion experience convinced them otherwise.

John was an assistant production manager in a publishing house in New York. His story is one of a clean-cut, fine young man who had been reared in the church. One of many people who have been led to believe that church affiliation alone assures them of personal salvation, John recalled hearing Billy Graham say that being born in the church doesn't make one a Christian any more than being born in a garage makes one an automobile. John certainly felt as though he had been born in the church, for he could not remember a time when he had not been active in church work.

As a Sunday school teacher, John was in a place of spiritual leadership. He became assistant secretary of the Sunday school and then song leader. Not only was John an active leader in the church; he had also begun to date a fine Christian young woman. He was attracted to her because of a quality of inner joy that she radiated.

Religious activity, however, could not ensure complete satisfaction in John's life. As he became more uneasy and restless, he began to seek for the inner peace that had eluded him in spite of his constant good works. Then John heard about a Billy Graham crusade. Someone in his church asked for volunteers for the crusade choir. John volunteered but did not dream that this association would bring about such a transformation in his life. He signed up to sing three nights a week.

"I realized from the first night that although I was active in the church, I had a great need," John said later. "Then one night Billy preached on the necessity of the 'new birth.' He told what a good, religious man Nicodemus was. Everything he said about Nicodemus could have been said about me. I had read that chapter in John many times, but it never had done for me what it did that night. I realized that there is no substitute for being born again. All of my church activity would not be pleasing to God so long as I failed to receive Jesus Christ as my personal Savior.

"I never did really resist God," he continued. "Even from the first night in the choir I listened with a desire to discover the secret of happiness and joy. When I discovered it was obtained by the way of repentance and faith, I responded to the invitation with others. Though I had promised to sing in the choir only three nights a week, I just couldn't miss a night. My decision was definite for Christ and my doubts were removed. I was sure."

John told how he and his friends had planned a full summer and how all his plans had to change. His desire to be in the meetings at the Garden took precedence over all other activities for the rest of the summer. At first he found that his family and friends thought he was becoming a religious fanatic. They felt that his good life and church activity had been sufficient. At home he had always been a good son and a wonderful friend. But John had found the assurance of salvation without which there is no abiding peace. He had come to know beyond doubt that he belonged to Christ. It was not long before his parents and other friends and relatives followed John to the Savior, and they, too, discovered that the formalities of religion do not afford inward peace. Only in Jesus Christ did they finally discover the spontaneous joy that overflows to bless others.

John's story could be repeated endlessly with certain variations. Of the 58,000 persons who came to the Savior during the weeks of the crusade in Madison Square Garden, approximately 60 percent had been churchgoers. Some were active church members, as John was, while others attended services only occasionally. Some had been in churches where there was little more than passing mention of the Bible, while others had indicated they had already had intensive Bible teaching. If anything is apparent from the study of the record, it is that one can know little or much about God and religion, but unless there is a decisive commitment to Christ in an act of repentance and faith, there is no salvation. As the Scriptures say, "He that hath the Son hath life; and he that hath not the Son of God hath not life." [1]

From the other side of the globe, in Calcutta, India, comes the testimony of Mr. and Mrs. Arthur Radford. Originally from England, the Radfords had lived in India for twenty-five years, captivated by the flavor of the culture. A successful businessman for these twenty-five years, Radford had just suffered severe business losses when he heard about a Billy Graham rally to be held in the gardens adjoining St. James Cathedral.

Although the Radfords had been brought up in the Anglican church, they had done little in the way of practicing their religious training. Since coming to Calcutta, they had not been to church at all. Curious about the Billy Graham crusade in London's Harringay Arena, about which he had read a great deal in the newspapers, Radford decided to attend the rally.

"I was convinced," said Arthur, "as soon as Billy Graham began to speak, that he had been sent to Calcutta for this very hour. Never in my life had I been searching for something to hold on to as much as then. He spoke directly from the Bible, and I had expected him to give us some of his personal opinions and thoughts on the growing world problems. What made the greatest impression on me that day was the way he explained how a person has to accept Jesus.

"I can never say that I had rejected the Bible. I just never bothered with it. I can't even say that I didn't believe in Jesus. I think I did. Like many British people, I took all this for granted. I even thought I was a Christian, because in India you are either Hindu, Mohammedan, or Christian. I was therefore a Christian because I was neither Hindu nor Mohammedan.

"As Billy Graham explained that a person must receive Jesus as a definite decision, I was at first upset. I took it that he was telling me that I hadn't been a Christian all these years. It was hard for me because I had always thought of Christianity as being superior to the other great religions and that I was a Christian. The best thing that could have happened to me that day did actually happen. I found out that I wasn't and never had been a Christian. I guess until a person finds that out, he hasn't a chance of knowing the Lord.

"The way things are now, I don't know where we go from here. I'm glad that in such a time in our lives, I found the real source of strength. In fact, I'm not afraid of the future at all. When I answered the call that day, it changed my whole attitude toward life. When I answered the invitation, it was not at first that I felt so great a need, but I felt that if I didn't go, it would be as if I had rejected Christ."

Mrs. Radford reported, "I could tell the difference as soon as Arthur came home. I hadn't been feeling well, so I didn't go to the crusade that day, but when I saw the look of deep joy on his face, I wished that I had gone. It's strange how life is. As a young girl, I had always felt religion was a wonderful thing. But when I married Arthur, we just left God out of our lives. Ours was a life of parties and social activity. We have learned that this kind of life never does satisfy over a period of years. As we have grown older, we have come to see that happiness is an elusive thing.

"Well, Arthur couldn't wait to tell me about the wonderful meeting and the inspiring message. He told me how he had gone forward and then he showed me some verses from the Bible. The change in his life and the things I saw in the Bible for the first time made me want just what he had. The change took place in my life immediately, just as it had in his life."

"All my life I have been associated with the church." This statement is a familiar one among so many men and women who come forward at Graham's crusades. If there is one thing that is true of the Christian life, it is that the church alone cannot save; only Christ can deliver a soul from the guilt and penalty of sin.

At the age of twenty-six Tom had already made a success of his career in sales. His ambition and charisma had endowed him with a natural talent for dealing with people. Because his parents were church people, Tom had been a member of the youth fellowship in high school and had taught Sunday school in college. In spite of his commitment to church activities, Tom admitted that, "I had never opened the Bible. Like many persons who are active in religious work, I thought I was a Christian. I really didn't know what the word meant. To me the matter of being a Christian was to follow a certain ethical pattern. I can see now that it isn't possible to do it that way. You have to have some power to overcome temptation and to keep you from slipping into sins of all kinds."

It was during his college years that Tom's temper began to become a real problem in his life, eventually getting him dismissed from the university. Joining the army, Tom began to discover that he felt spiritually empty and afraid. Through a series of "coincidences," he eventually ended up attending meetings in one of Graham's major crusades. Tom says, "I heard Billy preach over and over again. I was slow about making the decision; even when it seemed that it was the only right thing to do, I still resisted. It was a hard thing for me to admit that as a Sunday school teacher and church worker, I hadn't even been a Christian. I would have to face my Sunday school class and the people in the church and admit that I had been a fraud all the time. That was too much for me, because I was proud of my religious activity and influence with the youth in our church.

"From the start of the crusade," continued Tom, "I knew something was lacking in my life. I had gone to church because it was a good place to contact people. I was sociable and enjoyed such activity. I was afraid I was going to the crusade for the same reason and felt I was being a hypocrite. It's a strange thing how I finally came to make definite the decision. I recall a certain Saturday night. . . . My feelings were mixed. . . . It made me angry to have him call me a sinner. I knew I was a sinner, but who was he to call me one? I still resisted his preaching . . . . But my time had come. That night I felt I couldn't go on as I had been. . . . I was afraid that the next day I would be just the same as I had always been. I couldn't believe that such a change would actually take place and make me have new thoughts and desires. But the next day, I knew that a great thing had happened to me. I *was* born again.

"That was the best thing that ever happened to me," Tom concluded. "I'm never alone any more, and I always know that there is One who is interested in me and who cares."

Another testimony comes from the chairman of a rally held in Delhi, India. A member in good standing of the Syrian Orthodox church and a highly respected leader of Indian society, Poonan thought of himself as a genuine Christian and was perceived as such by all who knew him. On the day of the rally he was responsible for making opening remarks and for delivering the offertory prayer. As the invitation to come forward was extended by Graham, however, Poonan found himself joining those who were answering the call to become Christians.

"It was a humbling experience," he recalls. "There I was in the company of cabinet ministers and government officials, yet I felt I had to identify myself with those who had not been Christians before this time. I had to acknowledge my need of a Savior though I had been identified with the church. I had always thought that I was born a Christian.

"That night was a turning point. I didn't have any great emotional feeling, nor did I experience any drastic change. It has rather been a steady growth as I have studied the Bible and worked among Christians spreading the gospel here in Delhi.

"Before that night when Billy Graham spoke so clearly and simply about Christ and salvation, I cannot say I ever had refused Christ. I was always interested in the church and active in its work."

Our final story is that of a young bank executive named Srini, also living in India. He had attended a Bible school as a child and had read portions of the Bible. "Christ was a great teacher and social leader," states Srini. "That was the way he had been presented to me. A teacher had told me how Christ worshiped God and therefore I should. It was not thought necessary to believe in Christ but to be religious, as they told me that Christ was."

Eventually disillusioned with the life pathway he had been following and having dabbled in a number of different religions, Srini attended a crusade meeting at the request of a friend. Some 10,000 people from as far away as 1,200 miles had come to take part in the service. When the invitation came at the close of Graham's direct, simple message, 600 people stood to declare their desire to know and receive Christ. Srini was among them. "This was the first time I had listened to Bible preaching and the first time I had heard the words of Jesus, 'I am the way, the truth, and the life.' I had been searching for 'the Way' and many had tried to show me a way that a man could follow, but Jesus said, 'I am the way.'"

Chapter Seven

Conversion and the Church

The Danish philosopher Sören Kierkegaard once said of the established church of his country that it reminded him of tea made from tea leaves that had been steeped at least three times. Surely this observation could be made of the insipid and lukewarm spiritual life found in conventionally "Christian" churches around the world. If this is the case, it is no wonder that many nominally Christian churches do not understand or experience conversion and may find themselves at odds with the message and crusades of Billy Graham.

The church began approximately 2,000 years ago when some 3,000 penitents, mainly Jewish, acknowledged Jesus Christ as the long awaited Messiah, the Savior of the world. Having accepted Christian baptism, they constituted the first church in Jerusalem. Since that time, non-Christians the world over have come into the church by means of conversion. Indeed, the entire history of Christianity demonstrates that the experience of conversion has been the accepted way of bringing men, women, and children into the fellowship of the church. So crucial is conversion for the church that without it the church could never have come into being, let alone have continued its existence for 2,000 years. Writing about the nature of the conversion experience and its relationship to the church, S. W. Powell has noted, "Some denominations live by generation . . . evangelical churches live by regeneration. Unless men are born of the Spirit, evangelical churches will cease to exist."[1]

Having noted that some kind of lasting conversion is indispensable to the origin and growth of the church, we may ask how these conversions take place today. Certainly by means of the ministry of the Word through the outreach of worldwide evangelical churches, but genuine conversion also takes place in evangelistic rallies such as Billy Graham crusades. The record shows that, to date, more than two million people have met Jesus Christ through Graham's crusades. Although some of these conversions have been dramatic and have themselves constituted a witness to bring others to Christ, the majority of them have been relatively quiet and uneventful, but genuine and enduring, transformations. The church from the beginning has witnessed to the fact that these transformations are far more than a mere psychological phenomenon reducible to scientific analysis and explanation. Rather, conversion results from a person's response to the announcement of God's provision for those who were "dead in trespasses and sins,"[2] whereby they might be made alive to God through faith in Christ.

Just as the church must struggle with the need for conversion in the face of the human tendency to reduce religion to a set of moral habits, so must religious education. Elmer Clark has written:

> Certainly nothing could be more important than the formation of moral habits, but such habits do not constitute religion. Most religious persons believe that moral habits are not likely to be successfully cultivated among a very large section of the population save as they are grounded in, and motivated by, religious faith and sanctions. Though moral actions and religion have always been intimately related, they have never been identified by persons authorized to speak for religion. . . .
>
> Religious education is in danger of forgetting the power and need of conversion, defined as reclamation by an emotional cataclysm.[3]

Some psychologists and theologians have expressed the view that eventually religious training may replace the crisis of conversion. T. H. Hughes, for example, has written in his *New Psychology and the Religious Experience*:

> Not in vain is the Spirit of Christ working in man. He is making man a new creature and that new nature must be transmitted so that it will be natural, as it is now in many cases, for the spirits of the children of truly Christian parents to open to Christ as the flowers open to the sun.[4]

Such a possibility seems remote, however, for the history of the church has consistently demonstrated that an otherwise dormant church has been renewed by revival, by individual conversion, rather than by efficient and effective methods of pedagogy. Kenneth Latourette has expressed the mystery of the church's perennial energy: "Always the faith seems dying, yet it lives."[5]

The Billy Graham Crusades and the Church

Given that conversion is the means by which the church grows and receives fresh life, let's take a look at the relationship between the Billy Graham crusades and the church—at church participation in the rallies and the rallies' subsequent effects on the churches themselves.

In a random sampling of ministers of churches in areas where Billy Graham conducted crusades, the following statistics were gleaned:

1. How did you participate in the crusade?
    a. Preliminary planning
        Yes   73%
        No   26%
        No answer   1%
    b. Attendance
        Regular   50%
        Spasmodic   26%
        Little   13%
        None   11%
    c. Assigned responsibility
        Committee   10%
        Adviser   22%
        Other   4%
        None   64%

2. Did the members of your church participate?
        Yes   93%
        No   6%
        No answer   1%

    Percentage of those answering "yes" participated in:
        Attendance only   3%
        Choir   4%
        Bus delegations   16%
        Counselors   2%
        Ushers   1%

Attendance and choir   1%
Attendance and counselors   9%
Attendance, counselors, and choir   10%
All of the above   54%

3. How many inquirer cards did you receive?

0	1%
1-5	8%
6-10	14%
11-15	10%
16-20	10%
21-25	5%
26-30	4%
31-35	6%
36-40	4%
41-45	2%
46-50	6%
51-55	4%
56-60	1%
61-65	1%
66-70	1%
71-75	2%
76-80	1%
81-85	0%
86-90	2%
91-99	0%
100	3%
140	1%
200	1%
250	1%
400	1%

4. What percentage of the inquirers you assisted were already church members?

Already members	Reported by
0%	12%
2%	1%
6%	7%
8%	2%
10%	7%

17%	1%
20%	1%
25%	2%
28%	3%
30%	1%
33%	2%
40%	4%
43%	3%
50%	15%
57%	4%
60%	3%
67%	3%
70%	1%
75%	4%
80%	1%
90%	8%
100%	5%

5. Have you received any crusade converts into membership?

0	12%
1-5	39%
6-10	12%
11-15	5%
16-25	1%
36-40	1%
50	4%
56	1%
150	1%

6. Did any of the converts attend for a time and then drop out?

0	56%
1-5	25%
6-10	1%
20	1%

7. Do you know some converts who are attending no church?

Yes	25%
No	54%

8. What effort has been made to do follow-up?

None	14%

Visits	56%
Letters	4%
Phone	1%
Classes	1%
Visits and letters	7%
Visits, letters, phone	5%
Letters and phone	1%
Visits, letters, classes	7%
All of the above	4%

9. Did the crusade make a noticeable impact on your community?

Yes	51%
No	30%

10. Did the crusade make a noticeable impact on your church?

Yes	80%
No	10%

(Note that not all respondents answered all questions.)

Although the questionnaire results are straightforward and self-explanatory, it may be helpful to point out a few patterns which the questionnaire reveals. The majority of ministers who responded to the questionnaire indicated that they had participated in some preliminary planning and attended crusade meetings either occasionally or regularly. Over half of the ministers, however, did not assume specific responsibilities in the crusades. Ninety-three percent of the ministers said that members of their congregations did participate in the crusades—the majority taking part in a combination of activities involving counseling, singing in the choir, ushering, and participating in bus delegations. It would seem safe to assume that the factor of minister participation would have a positive effect on congregation attendance and participation.

Forty-two percent of the ministers surveyed indicated that they had received from one to twenty inquirer cards as a result of a given crusade, with 3 percent of the respondents receiving as many as 200 to 400 inquirer cards. Of the inquirers, 12 percent were not currently members of a church, 9 percent did not register a response, and the rest had been involved with a church for some period of time.

But how many of those inquirers actually became *members* of the churches which had received their response cards? Twenty-nine percent of the ministers indicated that they had not received any new members into their congregations as a result of the crusades, and 7 percent did not reply to the question. The remaining 64 percent, however, indicated that they had received from one to 150 new members, with the most frequent number of new members being between one and five.

With regard to the duration of the new converts' attendance at church, 56 percent had remained steadfast in attendance, while 27 percent attended only for awhile. (There was no data available on the remaining 17 percent.) When asked whether they knew of any converts who were not attending a church, 54 percent of the ministers said "no," while 25 percent said "yes." (Twenty-one percent did not respond to this question.)

Follow-up efforts with inquirers were made via visits, classes, letters, phone calls, and combinations thereof in 86 percent of the churches included in the survey, while no efforts were made in 14 percent of the churches.

A majority of the ministers surveyed indicated that they felt the crusade had had a noticeable positive impact on both their community and their church.

Problems in the Churches

It is a mistake, however, to assume that every church in a given community will benefit from a Billy Graham crusade. Many churches will not receive any positive effects because they do not have an understanding or tradition of evangelism. Because these churches are unprepared to participate in the crusades, they reap no benefits. Thus a number of ministers and congregations may report that no effects whatsoever were felt as a result of Graham's meetings. It is an unfortunate fact that not only do a number of ministers not participate in the crusades but they do not believe that conversion is necessary. In fact, a number of them do not even believe in the gospel. Anyone converted in a crusade will not find compatibility in such a church environment.

The majority of churches that have been positively affected by the crusades are those in which hard work and commitment on the part of both the pastor and the people have been found. Some of these churches have had an overwhelming response to their efforts. At an earlier time in the history of the crusades, researchers discovered that a number of inquirers and converts were not affiliating with any church because they had not been systematically contacted by church members. Since those early days, adequate planning and work with local churches have caused ministers to become aware of the importance of an intensive visitation program both before and after the crusades.

Appropriate nourishment and cultivation of new believers must continue well after the crusades end. In his aptly titled book *Where Are the Converts?* S. W. Powell has cited the dismay of many pastors who have been unable to see results from evangelistic efforts. One minister said, "I receive hundreds of new members every year, yet my morning service is no larger, no more people are at my evening service, and my prayer meetings don't grow."[6] Although this statement does not reflect the sentiments of the majority of pastors, it does speak for a number of distressed clerics.

Mr. Powell also quotes C. E. Matthews, late secretary of evangelism of the Southern Baptist Convention, who said, "The most justifiable criticism that can be made of all that Southern Baptists are doing today is their failure to conserve the results of their evangelistic efforts."[7]

Research has indicated that those churches with a record of incompatibility with the gospel message have not been able to assimilate converts from the crusades. These men, women, and youth generally leave a church that does not emphasize biblical preaching and go elsewhere. Often the ministers of such churches become critical of the crusades and refuse to accept any responsibility for their inability to maintain members referred by the Graham team in crusades. Individuals converted in the rallies have a strong desire to become grounded in biblical preaching, teaching, and fellowship. When they find a church that can feed them in these ways, they become committed to the minister, the members of the congregation, and the total church program.

Over the years it has been found that approximately 55 percent of those who go forward in crusades have previously had some church affiliation, and their response to the invitation is frequently one of a reaffirmation of their faith or an expression of a desire to make public their belief in Jesus Christ. The remaining 45 percent are people who have had no previous commitment to the church or to Christ. Thus, up to crusade time, these men and women have no history of affiliation with or membership in any denomination or body. Many of these people have developed over a period of time an antagonistic attitude toward the church as an institution. When they go forward in a crusade to commit their lives to Christ, they do not necessarily perceive their conversion experience as an opportunity or occasion to become involved in the church. They may view Christ as their friend, but the church as their antagonist. And so they experience their newfound faith as almost totally unrelated to attendance at a particular church or to affiliation with a specific denomination. They may feel that having found Christ in a crusade outside the church, they do not, at least immediately, need the church.

The discovery that one needs a church home and community may come slowly. I have known a number of new converts to remain outside the church for as many as seven or eight years. In fact, the trends discovered in our research show that of those who make first-time commitments to Christ, only a few actually attend or become affiliated with a church in the first year after their conversion. The numbers of people making commitments to specific churches increase each year from the second year through the fifth year subsequent to conversion. The apex of commitment is reached during the fifth year, however, and after that, the church commitments begin to taper off. It is most interesting to note that the antagonism felt by many toward the institutional church dies a slow death indeed.

Results of Questionnaires Distributed to Inquirers

A random sampling of inquirers who responded to a questionnaire distributed by researchers revealed some interesting results. The same questionnaire was distributed to four sets of respondents: those who went forward for salvation

(36 percent), for assurance (7 percent), for rededication (56 percent), and for service (1 percent).

Those Responding for Salvation

1. Prior to your decision, were you affiliated with a church?

Yes	57%
No	29%
Catholic and other	14%

2. Did you indicate that church on your inquirer's card?

Yes	57%
No	33%
Unsure	8%

3. Did the minister contact you?

Yes		48%
By letter	16%	
By phone	8%	
By visit	23%	
Through a counselor	1%	
No		52%

4. How frequently have you attended since then?

Regularly	76%
Frequently	8%
Occasionally	8%
Never	8%

5. Has the minister met a spiritual need in your life?

Yes	71%
No	29%

6. How would you measure your participation in the church?

Attendance	30%
Activity	43%
None	27%

7. If you are inactive, to what do you attribute your inactivity?

(Only about half responded to this question. Responses included: lack of confidence, dislike of hypocrites, questioning of one's own experience, an inexplicable drifting away, experience of trouble in the church or at home, health problems, nonmembership.)

8. Have you been different since you indicated your decision?

Yes	90%
No	10%

(Affirmative answers included: enriched personal relationship with the Lord, more peace, happier, hungrier for fellowship, more faith, an entire life change, more thoughtful of others, more Bible reading, easier to live with.

Negative answers included: went forward with the crowd, went forward out of curiosity.)

Those Responding for Assurance

1. Prior to the decision, were you affiliated with a church?

Yes	100%

2. Did you indicate that church on the inquirer's card?

Yes	86%
No	14%

3. Did the minister contact you?

Yes	50%
No	50%

4. How frequently have you attended since then?

Regularly	93%
Frequently	7%

5. Has the minister met a spiritual need in your life?

Yes	71%
No	29%

6. How would you measure your participation in the church?

Attendance	14%
Activity	79%
None	7%

7. Have you been different since you indicated your decision?

Yes	93%

No   7%

Those Responding for Rededication

1. Prior to the decision, were you affiliated with a church?
   Yes   89%
   No   11%

2. Did you indicate that church on the inquirer's card?
   Yes   81%
   No   16%
   Unsure   3%

3. Did the minister contact you?
   Yes   52%
   No   48%

4. How frequently have you attended since then?
   Regularly   83%
   Frequently   4%
   Occasionally   5%
   Not attending   5%
   Visiting other churches   1%

5. Has the minister met a spiritual need in your life?
   Yes   78%
   No   22%

6. How would you measure your participation in the church?
   Attendance   20%
   Activity   47%
   None   33%

7. Have you been different since you indicated your decision?
   Yes   90%
   No   10%

Those Responding for Service

(There were only two respondents in this category.)

1. Prior to the decision, were you affiliated with a church?
   Yes   100%

2. Did you indicate that church on the inquirer's card?
   Yes   50%
   No answer   50%

3. Did the minister contact you?
   Yes   50%
   No answer   50%

4. How frequently have you attended since then?
   Regularly   100%

5. Has the minister met a spiritual need in your life?
   Yes   100%

6. How would you measure your participation in the church?
   I am active   50%
   No response   50%

7. Have you been different since you indicated your decision?
   Yes   100%
   No   0%

In another random sampling of 527 inquirers surveyed over a number of years from a variety of crusades, the following statistics were gathered in response to this question:

> What did you do about your church relationship as a result of this experience?
> 1. I started to go regularly.   187
> 2. I returned to the same church.   140
> 3. I changed churches.   86
> 4. I accepted responsibility in the church.   114

The churches that converts select to go to are often chosen on the basis of relationships with friends and family. For example, Carl, a man converted in a Billy Graham crusade, was married to a woman deeply involved in the activities of a particular church. This church was one of the more fashionable ones in town, and the wife's family had been involved in its activities for many years. The services were quite formal, and little emphasis was placed on the central message of the Bible. When Carl was converted, he soon sensed the absence of Christ-centered preaching in the church and urged his wife to find another church home. She refused, not surprisingly, since Carl himself had never before displayed any interest in the church.

Six years after Carl's conversion, however, his wife also experienced the new birth. At once she understood Carl's needs and his desire to attend a different church. She, too, felt the lack of biblical preaching and was ready for a change. Soon afterward this husband and wife found a gospel-preaching church in which they could share in genuine fellowship.

A number of converts surveyed in the questionnaires we have cited indicated that they became more involved in their church as a result of the Graham crusades. One such young man, Henry, had already been active in his church, but as a result of the rallies he made the decision to take advantage of his GI bill and find a Christian college where he could study in a setting that would fully embrace and support the preaching of Graham.

Unfortunately, in all too many churches, even of an evangelical persuasion, most of the members have become virtually immune to the gospel message. This phenomenon is particularly true of certain types of families who have always shared their church experience with each other. Sometimes the familiarity these families have with the message allows it to lose its freshness and vitality. Eventually the children in such situations come to believe that they are Christians because their parents are rather than by a personal decision for Christ. Sometimes even converts from crusades return to the church they are most comfortable with and become like those whom Jesus described as "having ears but not hearing." Approximately 30 percent of all converts return to their home churches where some have an active, vital ministry, but others settle into a routinized life of stale religiosity. Only in active response to the gospel message can church members maintain the lively depth of commitment to which Christ has called them. Perhaps that is why Paul urged Timothy to "do the work of an evangelist."[8] Indeed, we might say that there is a vast mission field within the membership rolls of the church itself.

Clergymen often report that the spiritual renewal among church members was worth all of the effort of the crusade, even though some churches experience no additions to their membership. Often after a crusade a pastor is heartily surprised by the dedication and eagerness to serve which he sees in some of his awakened church members. Many ministers testify that they themselves have discovered new life in Christ and a fresh motivation for preaching.

Approximately 40 percent of all those who have responded over the years to Graham's invitation to come forward have gone on to assume responsible roles in the life and work of the church. Such a readiness to accept responsibility is, of course, a delight to the pastors in local churches. A number of ministers have shared stories of committed church workers who were converted at one of Graham's crusades.

A number of pastors have also pointed out the value—to both individuals and the church as an organization—of certain aspects of crusade preparation. The School of Evangelism, for the training of counselors, appears to have been a uniquely indispensable experience to many people. A particularly poignant example of the practical value of such training was seen in a Covenant church where a pastor had encouraged his people to enter counseling classes. Just a week before the opening night of the crusade, this pastor was rushed to the hospital for emergency surgery on a brain tumor. While he was an invalid for six months, his parishioners applied what they had learned in their "Life and Witness" classes. In addition to being active in Graham's crusade, they made parish calls on behalf of their pastor and became responsive, committed church workers.

Called to Preach

Approximately one out of every one hundred of those who have been converted in a Billy Graham crusade have entered the Christian ministry in one of its many forms. Of this number, approximately 25 percent become involved in some form of social service or become attached to a social service organization such as the Salvation Army. A number enter full-time teaching or administration in a church-related college. In one intensive training class in New Zealand, for example, four of the fifteen candidates for Salvation Army officership said their commitment resulted from a Billy Graham evangelistic campaign decision.

Those converts who enter the Christian ministry are distributed among a variety of denominations, some of which are not necessarily considered to be among the mainline brands of evangelical Protestantism. The majority of converts, however, tend to enter the Methodist, Baptist, or Presbyterian ministry. The more liturgical churches have a smaller percentage, but still a significant number of converts enter the ministry. Most of those who enter Christian service remain in the denomination with which they had been affiliated.

The Episcopal and Anglican churches in particular have an unusually large number of crusade converts in the ministry because of the exceptional crusades conducted in England. The Oak Hill Theological School, the largest training center for Anglican ministers, reported that, every year for twelve years after the 1954 England crusade, when students were asked how they had become Christians, the largest single block of responses came from those who had been converted during that crusade. Likewise, the principals of the leading theological schools in London indicated that for a number of years subsequent to Graham's 1954 crusade, 10 percent of the total enrollment consisted of persons converted and called to the ministry as a result of that crusade.

Inasmuch as more than three million persons have gone forward in all of Graham's crusades, we can conclude that more than ten thousand people have entered the service of the church somewhere in the world as a result of his ministry. Occasionally a member of the Graham team experiences an example of this fact firsthand. One evening when I was sitting on a platform of distinguished clergy in Great Britain, I discovered that no less than seventy of them had been converted in Graham's crusades. Likewise, I frequently have discovered pastors at ministers' meetings in New York who had been converted in the crusade of 1957.

Although crusade converts who are now in full-time Christian service hail from a variety of denominations, their witness is consistent. All of them first had their personal encounter with Christ while listening to the preaching of the Word of God at one of Graham's crusades. They experienced their call to service in almost identical ways. They have based their ministry on a preaching and teaching of the Word and are sharing it around the globe. Let's take a look at some specific examples of these full-time Christian workers.

George Thompson, a gifted portrait artist, turned his talent to painting pictures of Christ, and also became an officer in the Salvation Army. Another convert, the Reverend Warren Wiersbe, became a popular Bible teacher, having entered Christian service as an editor for *Youth For Christ* magazine. Another convert, a truck driver from Des Moines, Iowa, became concerned because one of the churches in the city was standing vacant. He obtained permission to open the church and began preaching. Several years later he wrote to the Graham team telling of the marvelous response to his preaching of the gospel. Of his past life the pastor wrote, "I had gone along with the crowd; I drank my share, I ran around." But when he met Christ, he found his ways changed. Today he serves God in a formerly abandoned church.

Another convert, Charlie Wise, a former teenage alcoholic, became a superintendent of a rescue mission in Portland, Oregon. Another young man became the founder of an organization for the distribution of gospel literature throughout the world. Popular in high school and regarded as an outstanding student, this youth had recognized that, although he appeared impeccable on the outside, his inner life was corrupt. As a result of being given a New Testament, he went to one of the Billy Graham crusades and gave his life to Christ. He writes, "I received a great power to do what I knew was right that I had not been able to do before. I was able to be that good person that people thought I was. I wanted to tell everyone that Christ was the answer and to read the Bible and to hear Billy Graham and to accept Christ. As I grew in faith, by reading *Peace With God* and other literature by Billy Graham, I started preaching at the age of seventeen to buddies at different club meetings, and God saved many souls in my high school."

Many more stories could be told, and many more testimonies related, from the lives of those who have gone forward to give their souls to Christ and then to dedicate their lives to preaching the gospel in one form or another. Without the witness of these individuals, the gospel could not bear fruit in the lives of millions of people the world over.

Chapter Eight

Psychological and Theological Perspectives on Conversion

The twentieth century has seen an explosion of interest in the field of psychology. There is an almost universal fascination in Western culture with the motivation of human behavior. Along with the interest in the general area of psychology, there has arisen a deep curiosity about one of the most inexplicable of human experiences—conversion.

There are at least two ways that the phenomenon of conversion may be studied. The psychologist may study it as a psychological phenomenon of a special type. In so doing, he is restricted to the observable aspects of the phenomenon. On the other hand, conversion may be studied from the point of view of the theologian. Both perspectives offer useful insights into the nature of the experience.

In spite of the growing interest of psychologists in the phenomenon of conversion, the church has failed to give adequate study to the matter. Nearly all systematic studies have been left to those who are either non-Christian in their approach or liberal in their theology. Hence, a humanistic and naturalistic interpretation of conversion has formed the bulk of the studies of conversion. This fact is indeed strange given that the Christian church has, throughout its history, viewed conversion as the primary means of church growth.

Meanwhile, the children of established church people have come under the influence of college and university professors who, lacking any vital religious experience, have convinced them that conversion is merely a psychological phenomenon without spiritual significance. Some of the more devastating declarations regarding the matter of Christian conversion have greatly disturbed many evangelicals. The upsetting pronouncements of a number of fairly prominent psychologists have caught many dedicated, but comparatively uninformed, Christians off-guard. Not having an immediate answer to a complex and highly technical problem, some have been silent in their witness to Christ and robbed of their own spiritual buoyancy and vitality.

As interested as the psychologist may be in making an analysis of the conversion experience, converts themselves are far more interested in what has taken place within their souls. Although many converts are unable to be explicitly comprehensive in their recall of the experience—or in an analysis of it—their conversion is, nevertheless, genuine. This fact has been indisputably established through thousands of testimonies. The conclusions of psychologists based upon inconclusive statements and arbitrary definitions are incapable of explaining the authentic, widespread, and enduring conversions witnessed by those who have interviewed converts.

The great contemporary interest in the colorful nature of the conversion experience has been piqued further by the disproportionately large number of converts in the Billy Graham crusades. Overwhelming numbers of people have also been converted as a result of the radio outreach, the film ministry, and such literature as Graham's book *Peace With God*.

In spite of the fact that a large number of conversion experiences over the last forty years have been associated with the well-respected Graham crusades, many secular psychologists have maintained their rigid opinions on the subject. They have observed the frequently brilliant and startling transformations that have taken place, but they have observed them from a distance. Thus, they are "armchair" students of the entire experience. Professor L. W. Grensted has described this attitude as a view of conversion "seen from an Oxford window." Even some religious leaders are guilty of this attitude, regarding conversion as unimportant or irrelevant.

A classic example of an "armchair" commentator was Dr. Reinhold Niebuhr of Union Theological Seminary. In the July 1, 1957, issue of *Life* magazine, he described what he called a "formula of salvation" as an "appeal to the Scriptures in terms which negate all the achievements of Christian historical scholarship." He further maintained that such salvation could never "include any of life's ambiguities." Characterizing Graham as a "frontier evangelist," Niebuhr maintained that social issues were being neglected in favor of an intensely personal salvation. He concluded, "A miracle of regeneration is promised at a painless price by an obviously sincere evangelist." All these comments were made by one who never observed the actual conversions taking place in a Billy Graham crusade.

In a perceptive article in the April 8, 1988, issue of *Christianity Today*, Bonnidell Clouse has provided some helpful comments on the relationship between conversion and psychoanalysis. In "The Cross and the Couch" the professor of educational and school psychology says:

> There are several differences between psychoanalysis and Christian conversion. Psychoanalysis brings unconscious processes into consciousness, where they can be dealt with by the ego. Christian conversion brings both the unconscious and the conscious into the light of God's Word, where they can be dealt with by an omniscient God. Psychoanalysis uses the method of free association (in which the relaxed client spontaneously says whatever comes to mind); Christian conversion uses the method of confession.
>
> One deals with guilt feelings, the other with guilt. One provides a release from emotional tension enabling the person to come to terms with himself and with the society; the other provides a release from the power of sin enabling the person to come to terms with a holy and righteous God. One brings a cathartic release; the other brings atonement. One puts the ego in charge; the other puts Christ in charge.

It is interesting to note that Christian conversion, so clearly taught in the New Testament and so frequently illustrated in the Scriptures and in the history of the church, is not characteristic of a given era of Christian history, of a particular type of people, of a specific denomination, or even of fundamentalists. "Fundamentalism" as a movement is less than a century old, whereas conversions have been taking place throughout the entire history of the church. In fact, without conversions, there would be no church. Those religious groups that disparage the kind of conversion taking place in Billy Graham rallies are, in effect, repudiating their entire historical foundation. Is not the

Methodist church of today the result of the ministry of John Wesley, who certainly preached with the goal of conversion and who witnessed it in large numbers? Is not the Presbyterian church the contemporary living monument to the evangelistic fervor of John Knox, whose courageous preaching resulted in a host of conversions? Is not the Lutheran communion an ongoing institution because of conversions that resulted from the forceful preaching of Martin Luther? Likewise, the Roman Catholic church has its roots in the evangelistic labors of Irenaeus, Chrysostum, Augustine, and others who preached in order to bring about the conversion of their hearers.

Interesting indeed is the allegation of some that the converts in a Billy Graham crusade are different from persons converted under other, perhaps less overt, circumstances. The fact is that conversion in a Graham rally is no different from conversion experienced anywhere else. There is actually only one phenomenon that can be scripturally defined as Christian conversion. Christian conversion takes place only in response to the gospel, even though such conversion may manifest the qualities of a psychological conversion induced by other means.

Studies have revealed that conversion may take place within the context of a variety of religions, and even within some anti-religious movements. As a result, some psychologists have concluded that all religions are equally valid and true, for truth is for them a subjective, rather than an objective, reality. In fact, however, conversion is so universally possible that we can easily conclude that, by virtue of being human, all men and women are capable of being converted. Conversion is not limited to a special personality type or psychological makeup. The biblical call to conversion is issued with the knowledge that those hearing it can be converted. The Scriptures not only presume this possibility, they also indicate that no one can ever become fully realized, achieving his or her potential, without being converted.

As we have said, not all conversions are necessarily "new births" from God. There are many non-Christian and even pseudo-Christian forms of conversion. But it is difficult for a psychologist working within the limitations of conventional psychological theory to distinguish Christian conversions from non-Christian.

In Graham's crusades those who come forward are called "inquirers," not "converts." This practice is in keeping with Jesus' caution to "let both [false as well as true] grow until the harvest." And he further indicated that the separating process belongs to One who is infinitely more qualified to judge than we mortals. Our Lord's parable of the sower and the seed illustrates the unpredictability of the results of preaching the gospel:

> And he told them many things in parables, saying: "A sower went out to sow. And as he sowed, some seeds fell along the path, and the birds came and devoured them. Other seeds fell on rocky ground, where they had not much soil, and immediately they sprang up, since they had no depth of soil, but when the sun rose they were scorched; and since they had no root they withered away. Other seeds fell upon thorns, and the thorns grew up and choked them. Other seeds fell on good soil and brought forth grain, some a hundredfold, some sixty, some thirty. He who has ears, let him hear." [1]

There has been a noticeable lack of agreement on the part of psychologists as to the nature of experience in general and religious experience in particular. Some ninety years ago William James wrote:

> When we talk of psychology as a natural science, we must not assume that that means a sort of psychology that stands at last on solid ground. It means just the reverse; it means a psychology, particularly fragile, and into which the waters of metaphysical criticism leak at every joint, a psychology all of whose elementary assumptions and data must be reconsidered in wider connections and translated into other terms. It is, in short, a phrase of diffidence, and not of arrogance; and it is indeed strange to hear people talk triumphantly of "The New Psychology" and write "Histories of Psychology," when into the real elements and forces which the word covers, not the first glimpse of clear insight exists. A string of raw facts; a little gossip and wrangle about opinions; a little classification and generalization on the mere descriptive level; a strong prejudice that we have states of mind, and that our brain conditions them. . . . This is no science; it is only the hope of science. [2]

It would appear that, unless and until those who are specialists arrive at some substantial agreement, one has nothing to fear when a psychologist attacks the Christian affirmation of uniqueness in the conversion experience. Nonetheless, the Christian who recognizes that there is a substantial corpus of psychological knowledge on conversion is bound to enhance his understanding and evaluation of the conversion experience.

A Survey of Psychologists' Viewpoints on Conversion

A considerable array of psychologists have attempted scientific investigations of religious experience, including such names as E. D. Starbuck, William James, G. A. Coe, G. M. Stratton, J. H. Leuba, J. B. Pratt, E. S. Conklin, and others. Although their sampling of religious experience is reasonably exhaustive, it is evident in many instances that they would have been greatly helped had they considered the theological implications of Christian conversion.

In 1902 William James published his now famous volume, *The Varieties of Religious Experience*. This work, comprising lectures delivered at the University of Edinburgh, today stands well above the other writings on this subject insofar as wisdom and insight are concerned. It is significant that among the large number of case studies he included, the preponderance are chosen from those considered to have passed through the evangelical crisis. In nearly every instance, however, James selected what would be called "the religious genius." The exceptional nature of the cases cited convince one that his aim was neither to discover the average conversion crisis nor to distinguish between the kind of religious crisis that might be induced by almost any religion and that of some particular religion. He failed entirely to discover the cause of soul-sickness, and his failure to go back far enough into these cases constitutes a signal weakness in this otherwise great work.

The "sick souls," according to James, are to be accounted for simply on the basis of a congenital difference between them and "healthy minded" persons, who are seldom listed among candidates for the religious crisis, the majority of whom are found among the "sick" type. The "healthy" type are usually in the group he called "the once-born."

These individuals are seldom candidates for the crisis type of conversion experienced by those whom James called "the twice-born." The "healthy minded" ones described by James were individuals whose religion consisted of a perpetual optimism and growth in insight and understanding. His "sick souls" consisted of persons who could not easily throw off the burden of the consciousness of evil, but were rather continuous sufferers from its presence.

The philosophy of "repression," introduced into the field of psychoanalysis by Sigmund Freud, has been one explanation of the "sick soul," or the guilt complex. According to this doctrine:

> Impulses, feelings, and ideas which create the conflict of which conversion is the resolution, are hot and alive to such a degree that they are ever striving to enter the conscious field, and are only held out by strong downward forces which have to be overcome if conversion is to take place. [3]

In those persons who attempt to escape from this conflict, psychoneurosis frequently results, or the kind of conversion described by E. D. Starbuck as an escape from sin rather than a "plunge into holiness, or into a higher ethical life in harmony with what is thought to be the will of God." According to the findings of William James, the result of this soul-sickness is that the person involved becomes one of the class known as "the twice-born":

> In the religion of the twice-born, on the other hand, the world is a double-storied mystery. Peace cannot be reached by the simple addition of pluses and the elimination of minuses from life. Natural good is not simply insufficient in amount and transient; there lurks a falsity in its very being. Cancelled as it all is by death if not by earlier enemies, it gives no final balance and can never be the thing intended for our lasting worship. It keeps us from a real good; rather renunciation and despair are our first step in the direction of the truth. There are two lives, the natural and the spiritual, and we must lose the one before we can participate in the other. [4]

James' study of religious conversions has formed the basis for subsequent investigations and has established a pattern. To appreciate his work, one must understand that it was not his purpose to write a defense of *Christian* conversion; instead, he was endeavoring to study religious conversion and experience, whether Christian or non-Christian, in order to understand the psychological phenomena which may be found among those who have had deep religious experiences. This is one of the points at which James has been frequently attacked by his critics. But it is only fair to note that James did not intend that his studies be used as a denial of valid Christian experience; no one recognized more clearly than he that the worth of a thing cannot be decided by its origin nor by a description of its function. As a pragmatist, he was more concerned with the fruits of religious experience than with its origin.

One may differ with James in his approach to the problem or his conclusions, and yet derive considerable value for the understanding of Christian conversion from the data which he presented. His description of the "healthy minded" and the "sin-sick" soul, as well as his later description of the volitional and self-surrendered types of conversion, may give considerable aid in the understanding of the great variety of reactions of persons confronted with the claims of God. Furthermore, James' description of the field of consciousness, the mental activity of a subliminal nature, and the breaking forth of unconscious impulses to the level of conscious behavior suggest keys which may unlock some of the problems of Christian behavior and evangelism.

One of James' best-known students was Edwin Diller Starbuck, whose *Psychology of Religion* is one of the earliest empirical studies of the religious experience. Starbuck's case studies focused largely on Methodists, as did Elmer Clark's in *The Psychology of Religious Awakening.* Traditionally, Methodists placed much emphasis on a well-defined crisis of a subjective character and endeavored to bring about such a crisis. Other denominations placed less emphasis on the subjective crisis and more on theological instruction.

The conditions under which the individuals presented in Starbuck's study were converted are worthy of attention. Of the 192 presented, 50 percent of the females and 33 percent of the males were converted in connection with revival influences. A few were converted at home after having attended a revival, and about 33 percent of the females and a smaller percentage of the males, at regular church services or at confirmation. Only about 20 percent of the entire number of conversions took place independently of any immediate external influence. It is also worth noting that Starbuck, in gathering data for the purpose of determining the age frequency of conversion, included, among the 1,265 subjects chosen, 776 male students at Drew Theological Seminary or among Drew alumni. The findings of this sampling of a limited segment of professors of the Christian experience convinced Starbuck and many others that religious conversion is a phenomenon which belongs strictly to adolescence.

In his *A Psychological Study of Religious Conversion*, W. Lawson Jones agreed, saying, "Conversion is a readjustment of the psycho-physical organism in response to the peculiar physical, mental, and social circumstances of the adolescent environment."[5] Another psychologist, G. Stanley Hall, also concluded that conversion was little, if anything, more than a phenomenon of adolescence.

Although this theory had been propounded as early as 1891, it has never been entirely rejected. It cannot be denied that later research has statistically confirmed the fact that adolescence is the time when conversion is most likely to take place. For example, in the Billy Graham London crusade of 1954, 52 percent of the men and women who registered a decision for Christ were in the age group of twelve to eighteen years. Of those who registered a decision in Glasgow in 1955, 35 percent were between thirteen and seventeen years of age. In the Washington, D.C., crusade 32 percent were between twelve and eighteen years of age. Such statistics are typical of nearly all crusades, and many evangelists and pastors have observed similar percentages of youth among their converts. However, unwarranted conclusions have been reached based on these statistics. Conversion in later years has been viewed by some as exceptional or unusual. Critical of those who have leaped to oversimplified or reductionistic conclusions is Robert H. Thouless, author of *An Introduction to the Psychology of Religion*. He states:

> It is to be regretted that most writers on the psychology of religion have been so captivated by the simplicity of the formula "conversion is an adolescent phenomenon" that they have often fallen into the error of supposing that this is all there is to be said about religious conversion from the psychologist's point of view. Their omission to consider conversions which do not fall under this formula is rendered serious by the fact that these exceptions have often been the most important religious conversions in history. A large number have been converted late in life; the apostle Paul, St. Augustine, and Tolstoy are well-known examples. [6]

Another psychologist who has made a significant contribution to the study of conversion is George A. Coe, author of *The Spiritual Life*. Coe examined the relationship between religious experience and personality types. Even a conservative view of Coe's data indicates that temperament has a bearing on the kind of religious experience that may occur in a given person. Christian experiences show considerable diversity according to individual temperament, as Sverre Norberg has also shown. [7] Nevertheless, it is probable that many persons have been led to expect a certain kind of religious experience for which they do not have the temperamental disposition. It is also true, however, that many people have experienced transformation without any expectations whatsoever.

Elmer T. Clark, author of *The Psychology of Religious Awakening*, conducted one of the most extensive studies in the history of the psychology of religion. Presenting an analysis of data on personal religious experience gathered from persons representing a wide range of environments, professions, and trades, Clark's efforts were directed toward discovering what an individual believed to be the *process* of his conversion experience. Based on his study, Clark found that he could identify three kinds of religious awakening: (1) the definite crisis type, (2) the emotional stimulus type, and (3) the gradual awakening type.

The definite crisis type included those who had experienced a real emotional crisis in which a marked change of attitude had taken place. This emotional upheaval occurred in varying degrees of intensity. The emotional stimulus type included those who had experienced a less intense emotional crisis. No special change was necessarily effected, but the subjects were able to look back on their religious experience with the feeling that their religious consciousness had been awakened. The gradual awakening type included those persons whose religious life had flowed like a stream, growing and enlarging, apparently striking no obstructions. Such persons recalled no period when they did not believe themselves to be children of God. Thus, there had been little or no change in their outer life.

Another observer of the psychology of conversion was Edward S. Ames, author of *The Psychology of Religious Experience*. Ames viewed conversion from the standpoint of what he termed a *functional psychology*, attempting a sociological interpretation of the origin, nature, and function of religion. Drawing his data and inferences from the findings of anthropology, Ames arrived at the conclusion that religion is essentially a conservation of social values in their most ideal and intensified form. He perceived conversion to be the result of the influence of mob psychology and hypnotism.

A particularly careful study of conversion was made by Alfred Claire Underwood in his *Conversion: Christian and Non-Christian*. A comparative psychological study of the experience as found in a variety of Christian and non-Christian religions, the volume presents a large collection of testimonies from Judaism, Christianity, Hinduism, Buddhism, Islam, and other traditions. As a result of his study, Underwood concluded that conversion is a permanent possibility inherent in the nature of humankind. As we have previously noted, this viewpoint is essential to an understanding of conversion, Christian or otherwise. Because of the intrinsic nature and consequences of conversion, Underwood recognized it as a valuable experience in the lives of religious persons. He furthermore saw it as a personalization of abstract ideals.

Writing largely from the viewpoint of an experienced practitioner of psychoanalysis and psychotherapy, J. G. McKenzie wrote an important volume titled *Psychology, Psychotherapy, and Evangelicalism*. According to McKenzie, conversion is any experience whereby an individual comes to be God-centered, whether the process be slow and gradual or a crisis of sudden discovery. Underneath the conversion experience, he maintained, was a sense of need that might include a feeling of dissatisfaction, a desire to get closer to the heart of things, or simply an awareness of an incompleteness stronger than any feeling of guilt or inferiority. The discovery of this sense of need comes in "the moment of vision," according to McKenzie. Subsequently the individual perceives a need for adjustment or reconciliation.

In psychoneurosis, says McKenzie, the element of the individual that resists reconciliation is generally unconscious. Thus, it is necessary for the psychotherapist to attempt to bring this resistance into consciousness in order to work out an adjustment. In the religious patient, on the other hand, a consciousness of the warring factions exists, and he struggles to resolve the conflict by removing the barriers to reconciliation.

McKenzie's conclusions have proved more similar to the evangelical conception of conversion than those of many other writers on the subject. He suffers, however, from the same ill that afflicts most specialists in psychology. His biblical insight sustains injury from an overemphasis on the psychological processes. These processes cannot be underestimated, but the psychological constitution of human beings provides only the material upon which the supernatural influences of the Word and the Spirit are able to make an impact.

Gordon Allport, in *The Individual and His Religion*, attempted to understand that portion of the human personality that deals with value judgments and religion. Allport believed that a mature religious philosophy of life was essential for the highest level of psychological and social maturity in any individual. Religious adulthood, he maintained, is realized only when a growing intelligence is somehow animated by the desire that religious sentiments not suffer from arrested development, but rather mature in proportion to the rest of one's life experiences. One might say that for Allport, the process of developing a religious sentiment is a kind of religious conversion—from immaturity to maturity.

To conclude our discussion of psychological perspectives on the born-again experience, I quote again one of the more satisfactory psychological definitions of conversion. William James wrote, "To be converted, to be regenerated, to receive grace, to experience religion, to gain assurance, are so many phrases which denote the process, gradual or sudden, by which a self hitherto divided, and consciously wrong, inferior, and unhappy, becomes unified and consciously right, superior, and happy, in consequence of its firmer grasp on religious realities."[8]

Theological Perspectives

There is a relationship between the true experience of conversion and the doctrine preached. That is evident to careful students of theological history. Dr. Kenneth Scott Latourette, in his monumental work, *A History of the Expansion of Christianity*, has observed in connection with the failure of heretical groups, "It is clear that the mainstream of the Christian faith has gone on through those churches which have centered their faith in Jesus Christ as God incarnate, as the eternal God become flesh for man's redemption."[9]

In his history Latourette wrote, "The Christianity which had shown sufficient vigor to propagate itself had always held to the uniqueness of Jesus Christ and had insisted that through him God had supremely revealed himself . . . for the redemption and transformation of man."[10]

Furthermore, S. G. Dimond has written in his *Psychology of Methodism* regarding the theological implications of the great Wesleyan movement in England in the eighteenth century: "Incidentally it may be remarked that every revival of Christianity has been a revival of full Trinitarian doctrine."[11] Thus the inseparable union of doctrine with evangelical conversion is apparent to those who have made careful observations as either historians or psychologists.

Except for recognized theologians, few writers have given serious thought to the existing relationship between doctrinal factors and conversion phenomena. Numerous psychologists agree that the conversion experience does take place and that its effects are generally beneficial. Again, Dimond has written: "A vast amount of research has been devoted to the subject of conversion, and it has been shown that, far from being a peculiar feature of certain forms of Christian revivalism, conversion is a fact of normal human experience, wherever humanity rises to its full spiritual development."[12]

Other observers have sensed that a close relationship exists between the doctrinal and experiential aspects of conversion, though none have fully developed this thesis. William James, who also noted the benevolent effects of conversion, wrote, "It is needless to remind you once more of the admirable congruity of Protestant theology with the structure of the mind as shown in such experiences."[13] This "congruity" is far more than accidental; it is designed. The perfect adaptability of man to the gospel is much more than coincidence. In fact, as we have said, complete integration of the human personality cannot take place until a coherent conversion experience has taken place. As E. T. Clark has pointed out in *The Psychology of Religious Awakening*, a purely emotional crisis can never be confidently held as true conversion in the scriptural sense. The fact that emotional responses can be experienced frequently and with varying intensity indicates that they cannot be viewed as synonymous with regeneration, although they may have edifying effects and some beneficial results.

Existential theologians and philosophers have rendered a service to the body of Christian thought in focusing attention upon the crisis aspect of conversion. Sometimes they have done so at the expense of the Scriptures, but they have forced the orthodox in theology to consider the experiential aspect of Christianity. Sören Kierkegaard, the Danish theologian-philosopher, said, "The way to Christianity goes through a decision in the temporal moment; faith is an existential leap."[14]

Emil Brunner, a primary exponent of existential theology, has written: "In his Word God does not deliver to me a course of lectures in dogmatic theology. He does not submit to me or interpret for the content of a confession of faith, but he makes himself accessible to me."[15] Such statements have provoked both theologians and philosophers to new directions in theological thought. Although there are disturbing implications in the existential point of view, it has at least forced theologians to reexamine their beliefs.

Conversion in the Christian sense can never be divorced from the concept of truth. In fact, to think of truth and Christianity as being in any sense separate is impossible. Christ's claim "I am the truth" was the most profound expression of the comprehensiveness of his Person as well as the clearest definition of truth. Furthermore, although the Bible has been scrutinized and criticized for centuries, it has not failed to withstand the tests of time; otherwise, theologians of intellectual integrity would have found themselves at odds with the Scriptures.

Although debates have raged over the years regarding the inspiration of the Scriptures, evangelicals have always accepted that "holy men of God spake as they were moved by the Holy

Ghost."[16] Having established the truth of the Scriptures, we must also examine our living *relationship* to that truth. William James wrote:

> If religion be a function by which either God's cause or man's cause is to really be advanced, then he who lives the life of it, however narrowly, is a better servant than he who merely knows about it, however much. Knowledge about life is one thing; effective occupation of a place in life, with its dynamic currents passing through your being, is another. [17]

Only Christian conversion brings one into such a relationship. To be sure, evangelical Christians have known this fact to be true, but it is gratifying to find a psychologist who recognizes the need of rebirth in order to gain insight into the things of the Spirit. H. N. and R. W. Wieman have written in their *Normative Psychology of Religion*:

> The mystical experience brings the minded organism of the individual into interplay with the ignored richness and fullness of the immediate environment with its hidden possibilities of meaning and value. It releases one from tensions and restraints, from the cramping limitations and blindnesses of the organized system of directing habits which ordinarily control the individual. As a consequence, there is a heightening of the physical tone. This affects the mind, since the mind is one function of this organism. There is new vigor and resiliency, renewed plasticity and sensitivity. There is increased power to reorganize, to achieve. All this results, of course, only if the mystical experience comes in the right way, and is not wrongly evaluated or sought. [18]

Certainly such mystical experience cannot be elicited by personal resolve or determination. That which is called the "new birth" is supernatural in conception, in implementation, and in final consequences. It is written in the Scriptures, "As many as received him, to them gave he power to become the [children] of God, even to them that believe on his name."[19] Or, as J. B. Phillips has translated this verse, "These were the men who truly believed on him, and their birth depended not on the course of nature nor on any impulse or plan of man, but on God."

It is scripturally true, as Graham has pointed out in his *Peace With God*, that "you cannot *think* your way back to God because human thought-life will not coordinate with divine thought-life, for the carnal mind is at enmity with God."[20] This truth is precisely what Isaiah stated in his prophecy: "For as the heavens are higher than the earth, so are my ways higher than your ways, and my thoughts than your thoughts."[21] Furthermore, says Graham, "You cannot worship your way back to God because man is a spiritual rebel. . . . You cannot moralize your way back to God because [the human] character is flawed with sin."[22]

Evangelicals have always believed that the initiative in the matter of salvation rests with God. The Scriptures say, "You did not choose me, but I chose you and appointed you that you should go and bear fruit and that your fruit should abide."[23] Jesus Christ is the living revelation of the initiative that God has already taken. The Letter to the Hebrews says that God has spoken fully and finally in the Person of his Son.

Although the Bible is a historical record of God's relationship to man, it is much more. It is God's self-revelation. Those who are converted to Christ are brought to the moment of decision and enabled to make that decision because of the energy of the biblical record, enlightened by the Holy Spirit. Thousands of those who have recorded their decisions for Christ in Billy Graham crusades are witnesses to this truth. The Bible becomes the final court of appeal in the crusades, and its penetrating power is experienced by multitudes.

A London attorney converted in a Graham crusade reported that Graham's use of the Bible was the authoritative basis for his decision. An accountant in the same crusade reported, "When Billy kept repeating, 'The Bible says,' I was convinced but I cannot explain why. There was power in the words he quoted." And finally, a suburban London homemaker, who indicated that she had given no thought to God or religion for years, said, "I cannot recall what Graham's sermon was about, but I was unable to disregard or forget what the Bible said."

Chapter Nine

Do the Conversions Last?

Since the beginning of Graham's crusade ministry in 1947, more than sixty-five million people on six continents have attended some 349 crusades, and more than two million have come forward to register decisions for Christ. These figures do not include the millions who have watched Graham on television; listened to him on "The Hour of Decision" radio program, aired globally on more than 900 stations; and read *Decision* magazine, one of the most widely circulated religious periodicals in the world. More than forty years of profound and far-reaching evangelistic ministry have yielded a rich harvest. The phenomenal success of Graham's crusades and the authenticity of his ministry are no longer questioned, as they were in the early days, but the question that has been asked throughout these years is: "Do the conversions last?"

An Overview of Graham's Ministry

Before exploring the answer to the question, "Do the conversions last?" it would be helpful to sketch an outline of Graham's ministry over the years. Although eight crusades were conducted in 1947, 1948, and 1949, it was the Los Angeles crusade in the autumn of 1949 that established Billy Graham. Newsworthy to the press and exhilarating to evangelical Christians was the fact that Los Angeles refuted the theory that the day of mass evangelism was past. Furthermore, the crusade generated new hope in languishing churches and new energy in discouraged Christians.

The new voice heard in 1949 bore the familiar, but half-forgotten, authoritative tone of evangelists of former years. Not only was Graham's tone reminiscent of great evangelists like John Wesley, George Whitefield, Charles Finney, Dwight Moody, and Billy Sunday, but the results of his preaching were similar as well. Graham's evangelistic style was prayerfully scrutinized as the team made every effort to avoid the errors and pitfalls that had often characterized mass evangelism.

The first chapter of Graham evangelistic history began, then, with the crusade in Los Angeles (an eight-week crusade with 350,000 in attendance, and 3,000 inquirers), and continued on a plateau of attendance and response for a period of approximately five years. The second chapter began with the first London crusade in 1954, a twelve-week crusade resulting in attendance figures of 2,047,333 and 38,447 inquirers. The expanded attendance, response, activity, and long-range effectiveness of this crusade moved the team's ministry onto a second plateau in the history of the crusades. The consistent dedication and singleness of purpose that characterized the team seemed to be ensuring the effective outreach of Graham's message.

The New York crusade of 1957 marked the beginning of yet another level in crusade history. Each new plateau of expansion called forth new prophets of doom, who insisted that the imminent crusade would be the beginning of the end of Graham's ministry. But the success of the four-month-long, massive crusade held in Madison Square Garden caused cynics to take another look at a phenomenon they had heretofore dismissed. The May-to-September crusade (extended well beyond its initial six weeks) drew 2,397,400 persons and saw 61,148 inquirers come down the aisles. Having moved into a new category of evangelism and broken previously existing boundaries, the Graham ministry began to be taken seriously, and articles and reviews began appearing. In a 1960 article titled "Theology and the Present-Day Revival," Sydney A. Ahlstrom said:

> In this context a brief consideration of Billy Graham is in order, for almost solely on his broad and manly shoulders has rested the burden of reviving mass evangelism and preventing it from becoming only a cheap and emotional accommodation of vague American yearnings or a sentimental reversion to a not-so-old "old-time religion." Not significantly realized, however, is his solitariness in the field and the drastic contrast of this situation to that in the days of Moody and Sunday, from 1870 to 1917, when the country was criss-crossed by roving teams of competing revivalists. [1]

The New York crusade not only generated evaluative responses in periodicals, it attracted large numbers of special groups who came to the rallies for the purpose of satisfying their curiosity about the increasingly famous evangelist and his message. Actors and actresses in particular came in droves to find out why Billy Graham, and not the Broadway plays in which they were appearing, were drawing thousands of people, night after night, establishing a record for attendance in Madison Square Garden.

An article in the New York *Journal American* noted:

> This was not a big sports event that jammed Madison Square Garden . . . with thousands more outside. It was not the wrap-up meeting of a national political campaign. No, it was bigger than these things. It was a great, devout gathering of men and women who had found God, or were searching for him and the peace of soul he brings.

Despite an expected decline after the gloriously successful New York crusade, the next major meetings, held in Australia, superseded even the Madison Square Garden attendance figures. The Reverend John Couland, founder of the Church Army of Australia, said, "Probably many feel as I do, that while Billy Graham may have been ordained as a Baptist minister, he has outgrown the job and has become, by the grace of God, an 'Ecumenical Evangelist.'"

Time would ratify Mr. Couland's judgment, for although Graham has frequently alluded to his Baptist ordination and affiliation, this tie seems to make little or no impression upon the broad cross section of church membership around the world. Billy Graham has for years been the unofficial spokesman for evangelicals everywhere.

The 1966 London crusade provided an interesting comparison when measured against the 1954 meetings. One single month of the 1966 crusade (called the Earls Court Crusade) saw more people in attendance and more commitments to Christ than the three months of the 1954 crusade (called the Harringay Crusade). Attendance at Earls Court meetings registered more than 25,000 nightly. In addition, closed-circuit TV crusades were held simultaneously in Leicester, Southampton, Birmingham, Manchester, and Newcastle. Adding the attendance figures from all these cities, the Earls Court Crusade figures soared to more than 50,000 each night.

The years 1967 to 1977 saw the expansion of Graham's ministry—with crusades spanning the globe, from Tokyo to Auckland, Kansas City to Zagreb, Johannesburg to Manila, Taipei to Nairobi. The total number of inquirers for the ten-year period was 624,473.

Since 1978 Graham has held crusades in such unprecedented locations as Poland, the Soviet Union, Czechoslovakia, and Romania. And expanded telecommunications have made possible an increased outreach via satellite centers.

Looking back over the years, we have seen some phenomenal statistics. Of course the yardstick for success or failure in any given crusade is the percentage of those who come forward to make a decision for Christ. A more accurate measurement of success, however, is the percentage that remains steadfast in this decision. Although there is no way to measure accurately and completely the percentage of inquirers who remain faithful to their commitment, the overall research of the Graham team indicates that between 70 and 80 percent of the inquirers maintain their commitment, while somewhere between 20 and 30 percent do not.

Those Who "Fall Away"

Disheartening as it may be to realize that some converts "fall away" and revert to previous life patterns, we need to remember that Jesus himself was disappointed when those who came near to him refused to commit themselves completely and irrevocably. Mark 10:17-22 tells the story of the rich young ruler who inquired into the life that Jesus had come to offer, but who went away sorrowful because he chose not to pay the price of discipleship.

Judas is another example of one who was considered to be committed to Jesus—for three years. But when Judas finally realized that Jesus' purpose on earth was not the achievement of worldly power and prominence, but the creation of a spiritual kingdom, he separated himself from the Master.

One day Jesus expressed his disappointment and grief at the superficiality of his disciples. The Scriptures tell us that Jesus had known from the beginning who of his followers did not trust him and who would betray him. He also told his disciples that no one could come to him unless he had been inspired by the Father to come.

"After this," says John 6:66, "many of his disciples drew back and no longer went about with him."

If the Savior himself knew the disappointment of uncommitted followers and superficial disciples who withdrew from him in times of stress, it is not surprising that a certain number of persons numbered among present-day Christian converts should prove unwilling to endure the rigors of commitment to Christ. Those in search of an emotional high, a quick fix for problems, or a hasty solution to a long-standing spiritual malady are not likely to have the stamina that is demanded if one is to follow Jesus without reservation.

Barbara was one of these inquirers. She attended crusade meetings for several nights. She had attended Sunday school as a child but in her adolescence experienced a strong attraction to the bright lights of Broadway. Eventually experiencing a series of bitter disappointments in her attempts to reach stardom, Barbara sought comfort through a religious experience and one night joined the hundreds responding to the invitation to receive Jesus Christ.

Weeks later Barbara was still experiencing an interior struggle. She wanted the peace of a new life in Christ, but she wanted to continue her old life, with her basic attitudes unchanged. Somehow she had overlooked the warning of the Savior that a person must always count the cost before making any commitment. Not willing to pay the price of discipleship, Barbara finally went away, tearful but unrepentant. She was numbered among those who had made a decision, but she never entered into the fellowship that believers know.

Something similar happened to John Chang in Hong Kong. A university student, John found that it was not easy to witness to fellow students about Christ. He had joined the inquirers as they streamed across the race track at the stadium one day when Billy Graham had given the invitation to receive Christ. Later, thinking that his friends would be happy to learn of his conversion, John was shocked when they ridiculed his decision.

Soon he allowed his witness to be silenced and he returned to his former way of life.

What had happened to John at the stadium could not be ignored, however. After three years of denial and indifference, he once again found himself in a place of repentance and surrender to God. Enough of the seed of the Word had been lodged in his mind and heart that he was drawn to reestablish himself in his previous commitment.

Sowing the Seed

The variety of stories found among the inquirers follows almost exactly the pattern that Jesus described in one of his parables. He told of a sower who went forth to sow. Some of the seed fell by the roadside and was devoured by birds swooping down on it. Jesus was comparing this seed to the Word of God that has fallen upon someone's heart but has not been fully grasped. The evil one may come and snatch away this seed, just as the seed by the roadside was devoured by the birds.

Then Jesus described the seed that fell on rocky areas where there was little nourishing soil. Although the seed sprang up quickly in shallow soil, the sun scorched it, and it withered away because it had no roots. This kind of seed represents one who has heard the gospel message and eagerly receives it. But because the seed's roots are not deep, it does not last long. The moment trouble or persecution arises, this person gives up his faith at once.

Still another possibility exists: Some of the seed fell into thornbushes and as the seed grew, so did the thorns, choking the life out of the seed. This seed is like the message heard by a man whose worries and cares, whose search for wealth, chokes the budding message so that it produces no crop, no fruit, in his life. There are a number of inquirers who sign cards after they come forward, but who return to their daily lives and become overrun and overwhelmed by the material cares of everyday living. And there are plenty of church members whose token attendance and superficial support present the appearance of promise, but who are easily thrown off course by the slightest intrusion of adversity.

The final kind of terrain upon which seed is sown is good soil—which produces a crop even up to a hundred times what has been sown. This soil, of course, is like the man or woman who both hears and understands the gospel message and whose life yields a rich harvest. Note that the parable says it is the same sower, sowing the same seed, who finds several different kinds of terrain that yield several different kinds of results. The ultimate results of sowing (or preaching the gospel), then, are not dependent upon the sower (or preacher), for it is the same; not upon the seed (the gospel), for it, too, is the same; but upon the soil (the hearer)—different in each instance. The audience, not the message or the preacher, constitutes the variable. The same preacher, preaching the same gospel, will convert some and not others. Some will go away as unchanged as if they had never heard the Word at all. At the same time that there are those who listen with attentive ears and respond joyfully and repentantly, there are others who reject every attempt of the Holy Spirit to speak to them. To those who respond comes the experience described in the Scriptures: "If any man hear my voice, and open the door, I will come in to him, and will sup with him, and he with me." [2]

The Research on the Converts

Gathering information on the staying power of converts has been an extensive, lengthy, and enlightening task. Over a period of approximately thirty years, 15,000 questionnaires, letters, and interviews (in person and by telephone), both solicited and unsolicited, have formed the basis of a study that provides an answer to the question "Do Billy Graham converts last?" A copy of the questionnaire follows:

MY CONVERSION STORY

Name_____ Age _____
Occupation _____
Address _____

1. When did you make your decision?_____

2. What religious influences, if any, did you have before you made your decision?
    Mother   Father   Friends   Church   Other
3. Did you ever read or study the Bible? If so, how much?___
    Systematic study_____Random reading_____
4. How did you first hear about Billy Graham?_____
5. Before your decision to receive Christ, did you think you were a Christian?_____
6. Can you remember anything that made you think about your need of God and salvation?_____
7. What kind of a decision did you make?
    Salvation_____ Assurance_____ Surrender_____
8. Why did you attend the Billy Graham crusade?_____
9. Did you make your decision because
    a. You heard Graham on the radio,
    b. You saw him on TV,
    c. You went to a crusade,
    d. You read a book,
    e. Other?_____
10. Describe with detail your life before you made your decision, telling about moral and spiritual failures of human interest.
11. What difference did you notice as the result of the decision?
12. Can you recall any teaching you received from Billy Graham that impressed you and made you want to become a Christian?
13. Describe as fully as possible just how you felt during the service, or while you listened to the radio, or read a book.
    a. Indifferent
    b. Worried
    c. Afraid
    d. Angry
    e. Guilty
14. When you came to the moment of making a decision with respect to your relationship to the Savior, how did you feel?
15. Describe your feelings afterward.
    a. Joy
    b. Relief
    c. Clean
    d. Other

16. What help did you receive from a counselor?
17. Did the Bible, as Billy Graham uses it, affect you and cause you to make your decision?
18. What did you do about your church relationship as a result of this experience?
    a. Started to go regularly
    b. Returned to the same church
    c. Changed churches (If so, why?)
    d. Accepted responsibility (Tell what)
19. What have you done since then to bring about spiritual growth and Christian usefulness? Be specific.
    a. Bible study
    b. Prayer
    c. Witnessing
20. Have other people told you that they see a difference in your life? Explain.

Although a number of letters and questionnaires were received in random ways, organized, concerted efforts at eliciting questionnaire responses were pursued. The Harringay and Earls Court Crusades in London, the 1957 New York crusade, the 1958 Asian tour, and a number of crusades in United States cities were specifically targeted for research. Below is a list of domestic cities, the year that the crusade was held, and the year that the research was conducted:

City	Year of Crusade	Year of Research
Atlanta	1950	1973
Boston	1950	1964
Charlotte	1958	1959
Charlotte	1972	1980
Honolulu	1956	1958
Indianapolis	1959	1959
Los Angeles	1949	1952
Los Angeles	1949	1961
Minneapolis	1950	1973
Minneapolis	1961	1973
New York	1957	1958

City	Year of Crusade	Year of Research
Pittsburgh	1952	1959-1960
Portland	1950	1959
Seattle	1951	1959
Washington, D.C.	1952	1962

Research was also conducted internationally. A systematic inquiry process was pursued in the following cities:

City	Year of Crusade	Year of Research
Calcutta	1956	1958
Hong Kong	1956	1958
London (Earls Court)	1966	1968
London (Harringay)	1954	1959
Madras	1956	1958
Manila	1956	1958
New Delhi	1956	1958
Taipei	1956	1958
Tokyo	1956	1958
Toronto	1955	1967

The Method of Gathering Information

In the systematic pursuit of responses from converts, the help of local crusade committees, churches, and files kept by the Graham team on the inquirers in the crusades were all used. Personal interviews were arranged, both by phone and in person, and the answers were recorded on the questionnaire forms. In other cases questionnaire forms were mailed out to a random sampling of individuals listed on card files or inquirer lists. Of course the methods of research varied somewhat from city to city and country to country—depending on the variables characterizing the context. In New York, for example, approximately 2,400 people were interviewed on the phone and in person one year after the 1957 crusade in Madison Square Garden. This figure represented a random sample of the 61,000 who had responded throughout the crusade. The research indicated that one year after their commitment, 92 percent of these inquirers had remained steadfast in their decision to follow Christ.

In many of the U. S. cities where inquirers were interviewed, random samplings of fifty or one hundred people were queried. In initial surveys of individual crusades, it was found that these figures were sufficient to reveal conclusive evidence regarding the steadfastness of converts. In some cases, as can be seen from the previous listings, samplings were done within a year or two. In other cases, the research was conducted eight, ten, twelve, fourteen, or even twenty years later. The research was also continuously augmented and "fleshed out" through unsolicited letters received from within a few months after conversion to twenty or thirty years after conversion.

The London crusades of 1954 and 1966 were closely followed up, with 300 interviews being conducted in each case. The converts from the Earls Court Crusade were researched two years later, while the inquirers from the 1954 London Harringay meetings were interviewed five years later at a celebrative reunion called "Harringay Remembers."

The most intense follow-up consisted of a three-month tour of Far Eastern cities in which crusades had been held in 1956. Beginning in June, 1958, the research tour originated in Honolulu and ended in Madras in September of 1958. In Honolulu an entire week was spent interviewing converts referred by chaplains and ministers. Many of those who had come forward in 1956 were GIs. In Tokyo, the next stop on the tour, interviews were scheduled every one-half hour to listen to the stories of businessmen, students, homemakers, and others who had found Christ in 1956. One university student who had been converted in the Tokyo crusade had started a daily Bible reading attended regularly by more than 100 students.

In Taipei no records had been kept by local committee members, so interviews were set up entirely on a word-of-mouth basis as a result of conversations with Christian field workers. The Manila crusades had been followed up in an organized way, so personal interviews were easy to arrange. The Hong Kong follow-up had been efficiently managed by an evangelical ministry called The Navigators, making it easy for research to be conducted among a number of businessmen, refugees, and laborers. A local Baptist church had received a number of new members as a result of the 1956 crusade, so these converts were easily accessible for interviewing. It was also exhilarating to discover that the Hong Kong pastors had experienced a cohesive bonding and sharing that had not existed prior to the crusades.

Calcutta was the next stop on the Far Eastern tour. Converts among businessmen as well as laborers were located on the basis of word-of-mouth referrals. An old mission and a Baptist church also provided contacts for arranging interviews. An efficient, dedicated organization in New Delhi enabled smooth research in that city—particularly among executives in several leading businesses. It was discovered that the Band of Fifty, a group of committed, tireless young men, were continuing the work of evangelization in the city.

And finally, the Madras crusade had yielded a rich harvest. Converts, Christian workers, and leaders were found in abundance. Four young men who had been converted in 1956 were preparing for the ministry, and a fifth young Christian had taped Graham's Madras meetings and brought them to Bangalore, where more than 300 people had been converted as a result of hearing the gospel message.

Statistics From the Questionnaires

For the purposes of this study, a random sampling of 400 questionnaires was gathered in order to determine the steadfastness of converts. Three of the questions on the previously cited questionnaire were considered pertinent in ascertaining duration of commitment. Question numbers 11, 19, and 20 were seen as revelatory of the staying power of a convert's experience. These questions read as follows:

11. What differences did you notice as a result of the decision?
19. What have you done since then to bring about spiritual growth and Christian usefulness? Be specific.
     a. Bible study
     b. Prayer
     c. Witnessing
20. Have other people told you that they see a difference in your life? Explain.

The answers to these three questions revealed that, of the 400 respondents, 388 converts remained steadfast in their commitment; 1 had not; 4 were undecided, and 7 gave no answers to these questions. Thus, 97 percent of the sampling had persevered in their Christian commitment; .0025 percent had not; 1 percent were undecided; and 2 percent gave no answer. While the random nature of the sampling produced an average span of four years from the time of decision to the time of the questionnaire, a substantial percentage of the respondents had remained faithful for ten years or longer. And some of the most moving testimonies came from people who had come forward at crusades more than thirty years previously.

The sampling used was a global one, representing many of the major campaigns cited in the previous geographical lists that were followed up with systematic, organized research. The sampling also uses, however, some minor crusades from which results were gleaned in a more incidental, informal way—through unsolicited returns or referrals from local ministers who forwarded mail to the Billy Graham offices. The international cities represented in our sampling are:

Bombay
Calcutta
Calgary
Hong Kong
London
Madras
Manchester
Manila
Melbourne
New Delhi
Sydney
Taipei
Tokyo

Domestic cities included are:

Charlotte
Cleveland
Columbus
Fresno
Hartford
Houston

Manchester
Minneapolis-St. Paul
New York
Pittsburgh
Portland
San Francisco
Seattle
St. Louis
Syracuse

The sampling also represents a variety of ways through which converts made their decisions for Christ. They include: attendance at Billy Graham crusades, viewing a crusade on television, listening to Graham on the radio, and reading literature by Graham—notably the book *Peace With God*, which has touched thousands of lives.

In the Converts' Own Words

The quality of the testimonies that appear on the questionnaire sheets is moving indeed. Statistical tabulations are helpful in assessing the overall success of massive crusades, but it is important to remember that tabulations alone do not tell the whole story. Let's take a look at some of the responses in the words of the converts. In 1982 one woman who had been converted in 1949 wrote in answer to question 19:

In January of 1960, at the age of 51, God gave me the privilege of coming to the island of Trinidad and opening a home for teen-aged mothers. This has been my labor of love for my Lord and Savior for the past twenty-two years—wonderful years as I have seen many young girls come to know Christ as Savior, have seen Christian homes established, have seen our first babies growing up into fine Christian young people, have seen some of our girls graduate from Bible school, and at least one is in full-time Christian service. Yes—wonderful years, filled with the joy I once longed for.

A young man converted in one of the London crusades wrote:

[I experience] a fuller participation in Christian fellowship with a corresponding reduction in my innumerable selfish pursuits—a deeper feeling of love toward my fellow men and a desire to witness before my fellow officers. [I have] a deeper and satisfying humility which has helped me to begin to comprehend the infinite majesty, love, and wisdom of God and how each and every one of us sinners is loved by him with a patience unimaginable.

Another young man shared these words:

I noticed a peace of heart and joy unlike any I had known before, both in quality and persistence. I have lately noticed a far greater sense of qualifying right or wrong in my actions. . . . I know where I'm going, and I know who's going with me. . . . The difference is that now I have a center and a purpose to my life, and this center is in the present—that Christ dwells in me—at times it seems in spite of my sin—and is with me always. The future is assured, and, if I can only learn to trust in Christ for everything, its worry removed.

A woman from Indiana, converted in 1966 as a result of watching Graham on television, wrote this moving paragraph in 1982:

Everything was different. Life had a purpose—a meaning. I knew I would never be alone again. No matter where I went, or what might happen to me, I knew he would be with me. I knew I had been forgiven for every past mistake. I experienced real joy for the first time. Everything and everyone seemed more beautiful. Over these past sixteen years, he has taught me new truths constantly, given me more compassion for others, made me more perceptive. I still have problems, of course, but I don't despair. He gives me the strength to endure.

A Maryland man converted in 1977 wrote in 1982:

All of my actions are taken in light of God's presence in my life. It is hard to separate my will from God's, but it seems to become easier through time and devotion. The hills and valleys are not as much a part of my life as they were the first two or three years after my conversion. The peace of mind is more evident as time goes by.

A woman converted in a Charlotte, North Carolina, crusade wrote:

For the first time in my life, I felt that I really had something to believe in and that the "something" was the most wonderful thing I had ever believed in. Not that I didn't have problems, because I did and still do! I feel as if there is no situation in my life that can ever come to me but what God and I together can do something about it!

A Minneapolis, Minnesota, woman converted in 1961 writes poignantly:

I have never been so happy. I feel as if I have lost fifty pounds from my heart.

And finally, a New Yorker converted in the great Madison Square Garden crusade told of the differences in his life as a result of his commitment to Christ in 1957:

> Immediately I noticed that the "artificial" Christianity was replaced by a brand-new experience that was completely "alive." The Bible took on new meaning and my prayer life was changed from mere repetition to true conversation with God. Everything was new, even me. The birds sang a new song and the trees—the few that you could see in New York City—had a prettier shade of green on their God-given leaves. But most of all, my soul drank at the springs of living water.

In the introduction we cited a journalist's allegation: "Experience has repeatedly shown that the person who 'accepts Christ' in such circumstances as those seen in Madison Square Garden is very likely to lose his way." Thousands of testimonies, both in the words and in the lives of those who did accept Christ in such circumstances, speak for themselves—in statistical as well as story form. There is no refutation for an authentic and transformed life. Such a life bears witness to the truth of the apostle Paul's words: "In all these things we are more than conquerors through him that loved us. For I am persuaded, that neither death, nor life, nor angels, nor principalities, nor powers, nor things present, nor things to come, Nor height, nor depth, nor any other creature, shall be able to separate us from the love of God, which is in Christ Jesus our Lord."[3]

Chapter Ten

Evangelism:
The Challenge Today

It has been said of *evangelism*, "There is a restlessness in this word." Only one who is engaged in a ministry of evangelism can fully feel that statement. The evangelist lives and echoes the words of Paul: "I feel myself under a sort of universal obligation, I owe something to all men, from cultured Greek to ignorant savage. That is why I want, as far as my ability will carry me, to preach the gospel to you . . . as well."[1] For Paul, as with every true evangelist, there was no resting place until the ends of the earth had heard the message of salvation.

The New Testament contains two words that are both translated as "to preach": *kerusso* and *euangelidzo*. *Kerusso* means to cry out or to make an announcement—in the sense that a town crier or a herald would make an announcement. *Euangelidzo* means to bring glad tidings. The prefix *eu* means well, healthy, happiness, joy. *Angelidzo* is often translated as "messenger." Early Protestants were called "evangelicals." The Oxford English Dictionary tells us that it was applied "to those Protestants who hold that the essence of the gospel consists in the doctrine of salvation by faith in the atoning death of Christ, and deny the efficacy of either good works or the sacraments." Although the word *evangelism* is constantly being redefined, no significant substitute for it has ever been found.

As the church of today seeks to adjust itself to a rapidly changing world, it is constantly faced with the temptation to forget its origins and its glorious history. The church had its beginnings in an evangelistic program, and without evangelism, it would have been stillborn. God said to Israel centuries ago, "Look unto the rock whence ye are hewn, and to the hole of the pit whence ye are digged."[2] The church would do well to heed this advice. When Jesus commissioned the apostles, "Go ye into all the world, and preach the gospel,"[3] he was establishing evangelism as the basic activity by which the church should grow and spread its influence to the whole world.

Today the church is passing through a reevaluation of the concept of evangelism. Although the history of the persecution of the early church is familiar to many Christians, we easily forget that the church evangelized and grew in spite of—and perhaps even because of—persecution. Beginning with the twelve apostles, the early church grew to 120 in the upper room, where they gathered to pray. At Pentecost the descent of the Holy Spirit added 3,000 persons to the church. And after only a few days, that number had grown to 5,000.

So rapidly did the faith spread that Tertullian, a second-century preacher, wrote with enthusiasm, "We are but of yesterday, and yet we already fill your cities, islands, camps, your palace, senate and forum: we have left to you only your temples." Evangelistic momentum was gained with each succeeding generation, but momentum alone will not save the church in a revolutionary age. It is the power of the gospel, preached under the influence of the Holy Spirit, that alone can regenerate society, but such regeneration must begin with the individual.

In this, the twentieth century, many fear that the evangelistic task before us is too great. We remember the words of Edward Gibbons, who wrote of the Romans in their age of disintegration: "They held in their lifeless hands the riches of their fathers, without inheriting the spirit which had created and improved that sacred patrimony; they read, they compiled, but their languid souls seemed alike incapable of thought and action. . . ." These same words could be uttered about many modern-day church members.

A combination of factors exists today that militates against true and powerful evangelism on the part of the church. First, we live in an era of unprecedented change. The church has always lived through such times, but the sheer speed with which change has been taking place in our time often catches the church off guard.

Second, one of the words that most accurately describes our times is *secularism*. The preoccupation of twentieth-century men and women with observable phenomena and materialism has dwarfed religious concerns. This fact is true not only of the Western world, but also of the Eastern. India and Japan, as well as the United States, are experiencing the effects of secularism.

Third, having felt the effects of a rationalistic secularism, the church has lost much of its faith in the supernatural, in the transcendent. As a result, many denominations have resorted to mere moralizing, advocating Christian ethics, and improving social conditions. Although these things are not in themselves negative, they are powerless without being grounded in faith in a redemptive Christ. The greatest social reformers, as well as the greatest evangelists, have always recognized the vital relationship between individual regeneration and social reform. As Jesse Bader has so often said, "We do not have a personal and a social gospel. There is one gospel and one gospel only, and that one gospel is the 'dynamite' of God."

A fourth factor to be dealt with is the global population explosion. With births taking place much more rapidly than conversions to Christianity, the church feels the increasing urgency of spreading the gospel message. The demographic factor has influenced many churches to try and solve the problems of our times by social legislation. But again, to do so is to forget our origins. Jesus and his disciples formulated no social programs; they preached to individuals. Such an emphasis does not deny the validity of social programs and of legislation; it merely puts them in their proper perspective—as a natural outgrowth of regeneration.

In an almost desperate attempt to cope with the special problems of our times, some churches have decided that the gospel message itself needs adjustment. Although methods of communication are never sacred, the truth of the gospel message *is* sacred. It is a message that must be proclaimed with confidence no matter what generation is being addressed—and no matter how many people are being addressed. Evangelism is still evangelism—whether a crusade for thousands is being conducted, or an exhortation for three or four individuals is being given. And in each case the gospel is being proclaimed to the individual. Mass evangelism is often thought of as superficial, simplistic, and nonindividualistic. In fact, true evangelism possesses none of these characteristics. The famous preacher Dr. A. E. Sangster once said, "It is a wonderful thing for the 'mass man' to become an individual, a person even. Meeting with God does it. Mysteriously the awareness of our individuality emerges then."

E. G. Homrighousen wrote in *The Christian Century*, "Can, should evangelism do everything? Evangelism's chief task is that of initiating the encounter between God and man and of insisting that the other ministries keep that encounter alive in their work." In our time it is a temptation to initiate this encounter by attempting to be "relevant" rather than by merely proclaiming authoritatively the Word of God. To quote Dr. Sangster once again: "For people who *do* believe in God, evangelism is a duty and privilege so plain, so incontrovertible, that all talk of 'relevance' is a half-vulgar intrusion of the utilitarian in a realm where it cannot apply."

Although endless discussions have taken place among evangelicals about the most appropriate methods and techniques to use in the work of evangelization, there is no secret technique that guarantees results in the initiation of "the encounter between God and man." The strange, indefinable mystery that constitutes that encounter can never be adequately defined, let alone induced by a technique.

Today, more than ever, we must be aware that "go ye into all the world, and preach the gospel" has more than a geographical application. It is not enough to go to Europe, to Asia, to Africa, to South America, to Australia. Going into all the world also includes the world of finance, of politics, of education, of sports, of the arts. And those who go must have had a firsthand experience with God. "Evangelism can never be done by secondhand Christians," as Dr. Sangster said so well.

The church today must evangelize or die—and if it is to evangelize powerfully and authentically, it must experience biblical renewal. As Dr. Chirgwin pointed out, "Biblical renewal and evangelistic advance appear to go together. . . . A rekindling of interest in the Bible tends to go along with a renewal of active evangelism. . . . The 'sects' on the outer fringe of Protestantism that take the Bible seriously and base their whole witness upon it, carry on constant and fruitful evangelism."[4]

The truth of this observation has been established by the global response to Billy Graham's crusades for more than forty years—crusades that have preached the unmitigated, authoritative truth of the Bible. Dr. Edward Carnell has described the Bible as "self-authenticating." Its best defense is its proclamation. Dr. Chirgwin again reminds us, "From the first, the church regarded the Bible not only as a necessary source of its life and faith, but also as an indispensable tool of its expansion. . . . Evangelism and the Scriptures are so closely interwoven that it is practically impossible to disentangle them. The Bible is an essential part of the whole effort."[5]

If it is true, as Dr. Chirgwin has suggested, that "the New Testament writers were not just writing history; they were writing for a verdict,"[6] then authentic evangelism will likewise preach for a verdict. As John wrote of his gospel chronicles, "These are written, that ye might believe that Jesus is the Christ, the Son of God; and that believing ye might have life through his name."[7]

Notes

Introduction
    1. A. M. Chirgwin, *The Bible in World Evangelism* (London: SCM Press, 1954), 21.

Chapter Two
    1. John 3:4.
    2. John 3:3, RSV.
    3. John 3:2, RSV.
    4. John 3:5-7, RSV.
    5. Ezekiel 14:6, RSV.
    6. Isaiah 45:22, RSV.
    7. Acts 16:31, RSV.
    8. Acts 17:26-28.
    9. Acts 17:27.
    10. 1 Corinthians 15:3,4.
    11. Billy Graham, *How to Be Born Again* (Waco, Texas: Word Books, 1977), 148,149.
    12. Chirgwin, *World Evangelism*, 153.
    13. Ibid.
    14. G. M. Day, *The Wonder of the Word* (Westwood, N.J.: Fleming H. Revell, 1957), 213.
    15. John 14:6.

Chapter Three
    1. William James, *The Varieties of Religious Experience* (New York: Longmans, Green & Co., Inc., 1902), 189.
    2. John 3:16.
    3. Galatians 2:20.
    4. Mark 1:15, RSV.
    5. Luke 13:3, RSV.
    6. John 1:12.
    7. Matthew 10:32, NASB.
    8. Augustus H. Strong, *Systematic Theology* (Philadelphia: The Judson Press, 1907), 826.

9. Romans 6:23.

10. Acts 9:3-6, RSV.

11. Acts 26:18.

12. Romans 6:4.

13. Graham, *How to Be Born Again*, 151.

14. Ephesians 1:17-19.

15. Philippians 2:13.

16. 1 John 2:3.

17. 1 John 3:14.

18. 1 John 2:15.

19. 1 John 5:4,5.

20. John 3:8.

21. Romans 8:9, RSV.

22. Colossians 1:27.

23. George Smeaton, *The Doctrine of the Holy Spirit* (Edinburgh: T & T Clark, 1899), 185.

24. John 4:39, NASB.

25. Luke 19:8, NASB.

26. Matthew 4:19,20.

27. Cf. Acts 2:2-4.

28. John 3:3,7.

29. 1 Peter 1:23.

30. Acts 2:21,47;4:12;11:14;15:1,11;16:30,31.

31. Ephesians 2:5,8; 1 Corinthians 3:15;15:2; 2 Corinthians 2:15; 1 Timothy 2:4; Titus 3:5; Romans 5:9,10;8:24;9:27; 10:1,9,13;11:26.

32. Ephesians 2:5; Titus 3:5; Romans 4:25;5:16,18.

33. Hebrews 11:6.

34. Graham, *How to Be Born Again*, 162.

35. Acts 17:30, RSV.

36. Luke 24:47.

37. Graham, *How to Be Born Again*, 160.

38. Romans 15:4, RSV.

39. 1 Thessalonians 5:17.

40. Luke 18:1.

41. A. C. Underwood, *Conversion: Christian and Non–Christian* (London: Allen and Unwin, 1925), 11.

42. Billy Graham, *Peace With God* (Waco, Texas: Word Books, 1953, 1984), 147.

43. 1 John 3:1.

44. John 14:17.

45. Gordon Allport, *The Individual and His Religion* (New York: The Macmillan Company, 1950), 142.

Chapter Four

1. John Wesley, *Journal.* Standard ed. Edited by N. Curnock. 8 vols. (London: Epworth, 1931), vol. 1, 139.

2. Martin Lloyd Jones, *Conversions, Psychological and Spiritual* (London: IVCF, 1959), 15.

3. Graham, *How to Be Born Again,* 165.

4. Acts 16:28.

5. Acts 16:30,31.

6. Graham, *How to Be Born Again*, 166.

7. George A. Coe, *The Spiritual Life* (New York: Eaton & Maines, 1900), 138.

8. Reynold A. Nicholson, *Mystics of Islam,* 84, quoted in Underwood, *Conversion, 148.*

9. Underwood, *Conversion,* 149.

10. Quoted in James, *Varieties,* 276.

11. Romans 13:13,14.

12. Charles G. Finney, *Memoirs* (New York: A. S. Barnes, 1876), 7.

Chapter Five

1. Frank E. Gaebelein, "Introduction," in Robert O. Ferm, *Persuaded to Live* (Old Tappan, N.J.: Fleming H. Revell Company, 1958), 7.

2. 2 Corinthians 5:17.

3. Romans 1:16.

4. Ibid.

5. John 14:6.

6. Luke 23:34.

7. John 1:12.

Chapter Six

1. 1 John 5:12.

Chapter Seven

1. S. W. Powell, *Where Are the Converts?* (Nashville: Broadman, 1958), 5.

2. Ephesians 2:1.

3. Elmer T. Clark, *The Psychology of Religious Awakening* (New York: Macmillan, 1929), 155.

4. T. H. Hughes, *New Psychology and the Religious Experience* (London: George Allen Unwin, Ltd., 1933), 241.

5. Kenneth Scott Latourette, *A History of the Expansion of Christianity* (New York: Harper, 1945), 504.

6. Powell, *Converts*, loc. cit.

7. Ibid.

8. 2 Timothy 4:5.

Chapter Eight

1. Matthew 13:3-9, RSV.

2. William James, *Psychology: The Briefer Course* (London & Bombay: Longmans, Green & Co., 1892), 467 ff.

3. McKenzie, *Psychology*, 109.

4. James, *Varieties*, 166.

5. W. Lawson Jones, *A Psychological Study of Religious Conversion* (London: Epworth Press, 1937), 54.

6. Robert H. Thouless, *An Introduction to the Psychology of Religion* (Cambridge: University Press, 1956), 187.

7. See Sverre Norberg, *Varieties of Christian Experience* (Minneapolis: Augsburg, 1937).

8. James, *Varieties*, 189.

9. Latourette, loc. cit.

10. Ibid.

11. S. G. Dimond, *Psychology of Methodism* (London: Epworth, 1932), 142.

12. Ibid.

13. James, *Varieties*, 244.

14. E. O. Geismar, *Lectures on the Religious Thought of Sören Kierkegaard* (Minneapolis: Augsburg, 1937), 57.

15. Emil Brunner, *The Divine Human Encounter* (Philadelphia: Westminster, 1943), 85.

16. 2 Peter 1:21.

17. James, *Varieties*, 489.

18. Henry Nelson Wieman and R. W. Wieman, *Normative Psychology of Religion* (New York: Thomas Y. Crowell Co., 1935), 174,175.

19. John 1:12.
20. Graham, *Peace With God*, 106.
21. Isaiah 55:9.
22. Graham, *Peace With God*, loc. cit.
23. John 15:16, RSV.

Chapter Nine

1. Sydney A. Ahlstrom, "Theology and the Present-Day Revival," *The Annals of the American Academy of the Political and Social Sciences*, Nov. 1960.
2. Revelation 3:20.
3. Romans 8:37-39.

Chapter Ten

1. Romans 1:14,15, Phillips.
2. Isaiah 51:1.
3. Mark 16:15.
4. Chirgwin, *World Evangelism*, 63.
5. Ibid.
6. Ibid.
7. John 20:31.

Selected Bibliography

Allport, Gordon. *The Individual and His Religion.* New York: The Macmillan Company, 1950.

Chirgwin, A. M. *The Bible and World Evangelism.* London: SCM Press, 1954.

Clark, Elmer T. *The Psychology of Religious Awakening.* New York: The Macmillan Company, 1929.

Clouse, Bonnidell. "The Cross and the Couch." *Christianity Today,* April 8, 1988, 20-21.

Coe, George A. *The Spiritual Life.* New York: Eaton & Maines, 1900.

Ferm, Robert O. *Cooperative Evangelism.* Grand Rapids, Michigan: Zondervan Publishing Company, 1958.

——. *Persuaded to Live.* Old Tappan, N.J.: Fleming H. Revell Company, 1958.

——. *The Psychology of Christian Conversion.* Old Tappan, N.J.: Fleming H. Revell Company, 1959.

Graham, Billy. *How to Be Born Again.* Waco, Texas: Word Books, 1977.

——. *Peace With God.* Waco, Texas: Word Books, 1953, 1984.

James, William. *The Varieties of Religious Experience.* New York: Longmans, Green & Co., Inc., 1902.

McGinn, Mark R. and Foster, James D. "The Mind Doctors." *Christianity Today,* April 8, 1988, 16-20.

McKenzie, J. G. *Psychology, Psychotherapy, and Evangelicalism.* New York: The Macmillan Company, 1931.

Norberg, Sverre. *Varieties of Christian Experience.* Minneapolis: Augsburg, 1937.

Strong, Augustus H. *Systematic Theology.* Philadelphia: The Judson Press, 1907.